TVRs
Volume 2: Tasmin to Chimaera

TVRs

Volume 2: Tasmin to Chimaera

A collector's guide
by Graham Robson

MOTOR RACING PUBLICATIONS LTD
Unit 6, The Pilton Estate, 46 Pitlake, Croydon CR0 3RY, England

First published 1993

British Library Cataloguing in Publication Data

Robson, Graham
    TVRs. – Vol.2: Tasmin to Chimaera. –
    3Rev.ed. – (Collector's Guide Series)
    I. Title   II. Jackson, Anne   III. Series
    629.2222

ISBN 0-947981-81-0

Part of this book was previously published in 1987 by Motor Racing Publications in the Collector's Guide
The TVRs, which this book and its companion volume (ISBN 0 947981 80 2) supersedes.

Typeset by Ryburn Publishing Services, Keele University, Staffordshire

Printed in Great Britain by
The Amadeus Press Ltd, Huddersfield, West Yorkshire

Contents

Introduction

TVR is a charismatic marque which has survived, against all the odds, for many years. Not only that, but it seems to have prospered by breaking all the rules. How many other car-makers can be named which have gone broke so often, yet approached their 50th anniversary with such a great reputation? How many other car-makers have stayed independent for so long? How many others have resisted the siren call to massive expansion, to building huge new factories on trading estates, and to believing in their own publicity? And how many could have achieved so much while basing themselves in an industrial backwater like Blackpool?

The first time I set out to write a book about TVR, I intended it to be no more than a factual, blow-by-blow account of the way the TVR motor car developed from the first machines built in the Fifties. All that, I hope, *was* included in those pages, but an additional, exciting element crept in repeatedly, and in the most unexpected places. This is what I can only define as the 'character' of the TVR, a quality with which all the cars have been liberally endowed.

Writing my first TVR book converted me totally to the cheerful 'can-do' philosophy of building cars which the little company has always embraced. When the chance came to extend my knowledge of these splendid sportscars, I returned eagerly to Blackpool to start again.

I wrote my first book about TVR more than 10 years ago at a time when the Tasmin range was new and the company's future insecure; I was not sure that it would ever need to be revised. However, since then the company has changed enormously. Not only has there been a change of ownership, but a change of direction, massive investment in new models, and considerable expansion to go with it.

It was astonishing. In the Eighties at least one new TVR sportscar seemed to be announced every year, and a number of intriguing prototypes were also shown, then never seen again. In fact so much has happened at TVR in recent years that when the time came to prepare a new volume, I was convinced that two *Collector's Guides* were needed to tell the complete story. Fortunately, my publisher, John Blunsden, agreed. Volume 1, the companion to this book, covers every TVR built up until the end of the Seventies, while this book, Volume 2, covers TVRs built since 1980.

Even so, a fascinating narrative has had to be compressed in order to provide every important technical detail about the Tasmins, 350is, Ss, Tuscans, Griffiths and Chimaeras of the period. In fact, even at the time of writing, I realized that this was going to be a never-ending story, to which I would have to return in later years.

In the vibrant period covered by this book, TVR made many headlines, produced some exciting new models and defied all the pundits who regularly predicted commercial disaster for the firm. How many other car-makers could celebrate a period which involved the company changing hands in 1981, phasing-in a totally new type of engine in 1983, going back into – and later abandoning – the US market, developing 160mph-plus Supercars *and* deciding to develop and produce its own-brand engines?

Having survived a low point in the early Eighties, TVR production continually rose at the end of the decade, so much so that in the first 12 years following the birth of the Tasmin, more than 6,000 cars were produced – more than the total of *all* TVR models built in the first 25 years of the company's life. During the Nineties, and despite the physical constraints of the Bristol Avenue buildings, TVR will surely begin building at least 1,000 cars a year.

Throughout the company's history, the character of the TVR has always shone through, nowhere more obviously than in the engineering of the cars. Every TVR has had a multi-tubular chassis-frame, all-independent suspension and a glassfibre/composite bodyshell. Every car, too, whether equipped with a powerful engine or not, has undeniably been a sportscar, and TVR certainly can never be accused of providing boring machinery.

Therefore, is it any wonder that the demand for TVRs, whether new or 'classic', continues to grow?

October 1993   **GRAHAM ROBSON**

Acknowledgements

Whenever I tackle the story of a car or a car company, it is never easy to extract all the history, statistics and photographs without persuading busy people for assistance. Although most of the material in this book counts as recent history, much guidance was still required before finding the correct files and all the correct references.

My job, therefore, has been made much easier by the following experts:

For encouragement, personal help in locating archives, raking through their memories and advising on the content of the book: Peter Wheeler, Stewart Halstead, Martin Lilley, Carole Newton, Noel Palmer, Mike Penny and James Pillar, of TVR Engineering Ltd.

For their enthusiasm in maintaining interest in the marque, through thick and thin: the TVR Car Club Ltd and their principal officers, not least Douglas Manuel and Roger Cook.

In earlier years, for his personal involvement in all matters TVR, and particularly for letting me trawl through his impressive stock of historical records and illustrations: John Bailie and his staff at Image Publicity in Blackpool.

Those recorders of the automotive scene, for their archival and historical importance: *Autocar, Motor, Autocar & Motor, Autosport, Classic & Sportscar, Classic Cars, Road & Track* and *Car and Driver.*

My personal American connection: Richard Langworth, of Dragonwyck Publishing Inc, New Hampshire, USA.

Lastly, of course, I should acknowledge yet again the debt which all TVR enthusiasts owe to Arthur and Martin Lilley for conceiving the Tasmin model, the founding member of the modern TVR range, and to Peter Wheeler and Stewart Halstead for building on their vision. Through their persistence, I am sure that TVR will prosper for many years to come.

                                GRAHAM ROBSON

TVR have a long history of introducing prototypes at motor shows in order to gauge public response before putting them into production. This is the Cerbera, a 2+2 development of the Chimaera, which became a centre of interest at the Earls Court Motorfair in October 1993. *(TVR)*

CHAPTER 1

Ancestors and heritage

The growth of TVR

Although the story of TVR effectively began in 1947, when a young man called Trevor Wilkinson first built himself a 'special', the first TVR-badged sportscars were not sold until 1954, and series production of Granturas did not begin until 1958. Even then it was not until the late Sixties that the company became financially stable. What we might call the 'mature' TVR concern did not develop until the Seventies, when the M-Series chassis was put into production.

Although many different types of TVR have been sold since the Fifties, every production car has conformed to the same basic pattern. All have been sportscars built in Blackpool, where light industry rubs shoulders uneasily with kiss-me-quick hats, the smell of fish and chips, and with end-of-the-pier humour. Perhaps this is one reason why every TVR seems to have a great deal of character to add to its undoubted performance and agility. Almost all have been pure two-seaters, and since 1978 the vast majority have been convertibles.

Anyone new to TVR might be excused for thinking that this was a simple heritage, and that it would be easy to summarize. However, TVR has never been a family business, with father handing it down to son, and with one style evolving subtly from the last.

Changes of management, strategy and style have made a fascinating story ever more complicated. There have been times when TVR's future looked rocky, and times when production was suspended completely.

By 1980, when the original Tasmin was launched, and the narrative of *this* volume truly begins, financial stability had been achieved, and more than 300 cars a year were being made. It was a far cry from the Fifties and Sixties, when sales and profitability fluctuated alarmingly.

Small beginnings
Trevor Wilkinson, having completed a motor trade apprenticeship in the town, set up Trevcar Motors at Beverley Grove in Blackpool in 1947, and built himself an Alvis Firebird-based 'special' in the same year. TVR Engineering

Side view of one of the early series-production Grantura Mark 1 models, showing the stubby and completely characteristic lines, the wrap-around rear window, the smoothly contoured tail (contrasting with the lumpy outline of the 1959 Coupe) and the lack of opening quarter-windows in the doors. Already, however, modifications have been made to the original, for this particular car has exposed headlamps with chrome decorating rings. *(John Bailie)*

This shot, taken in 1976, gives a vivid and revealing comparison between the current model TVR 3000M Turbo and a 1961 Grantura Mark IIA. The family resemblance is clear, though it is obvious that there is no direct link between the two designs. The Mark IIA has been modified by its owner, for the single bonnet air intake was never part of the standard specification. This picture was taken outside the TVR factory at Bristol Avenue. *(TVR)*

(TVR, as many enthusiasts know, is a diminution of TreVoR, Wilkinson's christian name) was founded shortly afterwards, and the first multi-tubular-chassis prototype, complete with side-valve Ford engine, was completed in 1949.

More one-offs followed, usually with bodies provided by outside concerns, but the first recognizable TVR ancestors, with GRP bodies produced in Blackpool, were sold in 1956 to Ray Saidel of the USA, where they were badged as Jomars. This was the car which combined and refined all of Wilkinson's early ideas, for the multi-tubular chassis had independent front suspension (trailing arm/torsion bar type, lifted from the VW Beetle), and a much-modified Microplas bodyshell.

From 1956 Wilkinson moved his business to the Hoo Hill Industrial Estate at Layton, on the outskirts of Blackpool, where he refined the Jomar design and put the TVR Grantura on sale. By 1958, something like series production had been established, the TVR had been publicized in Britain's most influential motoring magazines – *The Autocar* and *The Motor* – and the company was on its way.

In the next seven years the TVR marque was often swamped in a maelstrom of financial chaos and management changes. By 1965, when production ended for a time, there had been two bankruptcies and several other reconstructions.

Between 1958 and 1962 about 500 Granturas – Mks I, II and IIA – were produced, all of them with the same wide-track/short-wheelbase (7ft) chassis, and a two-seater coupe body style which was to evolve only gradually during the next two decades. By the standards of the day, the Granturas were fast, agile and very sporting. To that historical view must now be added the fact that they were extremely hard-sprung, with cramped interiors, and of rather doubtful build quality. Complete cars were supplied, but it was also possible for customers to buy an incomplete kit, for assembly at home, and to save paying Purchase Tax.

At the front, the snout was low and at the rear there was a sloping fast-back shape and a vast rear window; at first, a wide range of four-cylinder engines was available. Then, as later, TVR made its own chassis-frames from a pile of tubes on very simple jigs, and its own bodies from glassfibre mat and on simple moulds. As the years progressed, increasingly more details – chassis, trim and electrical – would be added to the 'own-brand' list of components.

Financial upheavals erupted almost at once, with Layton Sports Cars Ltd taking over in 1958, Grantura Engineering Ltd joining in alongside in 1959, and poor Trevor Wilkinson being pushed gradually out of the limelight. New finance, from the Aitchinson-Hopton business in Chester, followed in 1961. TVR Cars Ltd took over from Layton Sports Cars, which was wound up, and the immediate result was the launch of a new model, the Grantura MkIII.

MkIII and Griffith – big ideas, but few resources

The MkIII was the first model to use a new generation of TVR chassis, a stiffer design complete with coil-spring-and-wishbone independent suspension. Although the MkIII looked similar to the MkIIA, the wheelbase was 1.5in longer and there were many other detail style changes. Even so, like earlier models, there was still no external access to the rear stowage area, which meant that the spare wheel had to be lugged out over the seats, through the narrow door, if a wheel had to be changed.

Most MkIIIs had MGA or MGB engines and transmissions, but although they were better cars than before, the management was not. Trevor Wilkinson walked out on the company he had founded 15 years earlier, a motorsport programme was expensive and totally unsuccessful, and TVR Cars Ltd collapsed before the end of 1962.

But Grantura Engineering survived, picked up the pieces, and started building cars again. In the next two years there were two important developments – one being the launch of the hilariously under-developed Ford-USA V8-engined Griffith (for export only), the other the facelift of the body style, which included a sharply cut-off tail.

Boosting production to build 300 Griffith V8s in two years stretched cash-flow to the limit. Ambition then got the better of the company, which promptly fell, when the current management team – this time funded by Arnold Burton, from the wealthy Yorkshire-based tailoring dynasty – overstretched itself with the stillborn Trident project. In the autumn of 1965 yet another TVR company closed down, and

The badge tells us that this was a Vixen, and the number-plate denotes a car registered between August 1968 and August 1969, while the use of those unmistakable tail-lamp clusters from the Ford Cortina Mark I finally clinch the identification – this is a Series I Vixen. *(John Bailie)*

production was suspended…

Martin Lilley takes over

This was the point at which stability *finally* came to TVR. Martin Lilley (whose Barnet Motor Co Ltd had become TVR dealers earlier in the year) and his father, Arthur, bought the assets of Grantura Engineering Ltd from the Receiver in November 1975, founded TVR Engineering Ltd – the company which builds TVRs to this day – and got the TVR marque back into business before the end of the year.

Arthur Lilley, though a major shareholder in the business, left Martin alone to run the business, and for the next 16 years the company evolved peacefully, logically and profitably. Although there was no need for any changes in corporate structure during that period, there was a steady stream of new models, a move to a new factory, sales expansion into the USA once again, and finally the development of a brand-new

The feature most often criticized by testers of TVRs was the poor access to the luggage space. This was finally rectified in 1976, when the hatchback Taimar was announced. With the hatch closed the lines of the M-Series car were virtually unaltered, but with the hatch open there was no missing the new feature. Ahead of the doors, there was absolutely no change to chassis or body, and behind that line the changes were kept to a minimum. *(TVR)*

chassis and body style – the Tasmin.

The gradual transformation of TVR from a financially-struggling minnow to a well-established company is covered in detail in the companion volume to this book. This, in summary, is how a marque building a few MGB-engined Granturas a year became a company offering three body styles and several different engines:

1967: The Ford-engined Vixen took over from the Grantura/1800S series, using the same chassis and style; a year later a longer-wheelbase (7ft 6in) version was introduced.

1969: The Tuscan V6 was put on sale. This was effectively a Vixen with a 3-litre Ford V6 engine, and was the first time TVR had used a Ford-UK vee-layout engine.

1970: The business was relocated, out of the Hoo Hill works to Bristol Avenue, Blackpool, where it remains to this day. This was the year in which the last Ford-USA V8-engined car of the original Griffith/Tuscan series was built.

1971: The TVR 2500 model (complete with de-toxed Triumph TR6 engine) was launched, and TVR began sending cars to the USA. A total of 360 TVRs were produced in that year.

1972: A new M-Series chassis and related body style was introduced to replace the old Grantura/Vixen/Tuscan type. A three-model range – 1600M, 2500M and 3000M – was established.

1974: Record production of 421 cars was achieved, 372 of these being 2500M models.

1975: A serious fire damaged the factory in January. Production did not restart until March/April.

The trend-setting Turbo model – 63 would eventually be made – was introduced.

1976: The first new TVR body style – a hatchback coupe – was introduced. Based on the M-Series, this was the Taimar.

1978: The first drop-top TVR, called the 3000S Convertible, was introduced. It was a great success in the USA.

By the late Seventies, TVR had established itself as a serious British car-maker. The Turbo and the 3000S Convertibles, in particular, had been trailblazers. Not only was the Turbo the first British production car to have turbocharging, but it also returned TVR to the standing of a 'Supercar' builder, a position which it had reluctantly abandoned in 1970. The Convertible seemed to be just the car that the market needed.

These innovations signalled the fact that TVR was now technically capable of tackling complex engineering jobs, which should have given their rivals cause to think about their intentions for the Eighties. For even while the Turbo TVRs were making all the headlines in the enthusiast press, TVR engineers were working on a brand-new car.

The result was the launch of the Tasmin, and it brought TVR controversially and excitingly into the Eighties. At a stroke TVR cast out the lusty Ford 3-litre V6 of the M-Series, the convertible body option, and a rounded body shape. Was this the correct strategy? We would shortly find out.

Turbocharged TVRs were very rare – only 63 were built between 1975 and 1979 – mainly because they were much more expensive than normally aspirated versions. This is one in rolling-chassis form, during assembly at Blackpool. The cylindrical black object near the chassis crossmember is an air-cleaner for the turbocharger intake, and the turbocharger itself is below it, hidden under the light-coloured panel ahead of the crossmember which protects the spare wheel from the heat. In the background is a mixture of 3000Ms intended for different markets – the picture was taken before the Taimar or the Convertible had been introduced. *(TVR)*

TVR 3000M

This magnificent cutaway drawing of the 3000M was prepared by John Bailie, a TVR owner who is also the proprietor of Image Publicity, who have close business connections with TVR Engineering Ltd. This shows the 3000M in its definitive state as the most successful of all Seventies' TVRs sold in Britain. Note the cylindrical fuel tank, mounted low down and at the rear of the car. *(John Bailie)*

CHAPTER 2

The Tasmin project

New chassis, new style, new engines from 1980

From 1958 to 1979, the development of the TVR motor car followed a steady and logical course. In 1980, the arrival of the Tasmin signalled 'all change' at Blackpool, for in almost every mechanical and body detail the new model differed completely from the M-Series. At one stroke, the Tasmin changed the face of TVR, and it is certainly the project on which the company's prosperity for the Eighties was built.

The design, development and preparation for production of the Tasmin was the biggest and most important project ever tackled by TVR up to that time. It took three years, an investment of at least £500,000, the complete rejigging of factory facilities and a great deal of corporate resolution to put the car on the market at all. Only one version – the Tasmin fixed-head two-seater – was produced at first, but within a year it was joined by the Tasmin Convertible and the Tasmin +2. With a further expansion of production, and with an eye to opening-up new export markets, more exciting derivatives were expected in the next year or so.

By 1976, TVR Engineering had recovered from the factory fire, were back in full production and were on the way to developing a full range of models. Not only were three engines – 1600, 2500 and 3000 – available, but the Turbo derivatives had been launched, the hatchback Taimar was about to be announced and the Convertible was under development. After more than 10 years of control at TVR, Martin Lilley was ready to consider a radically new model. The name he chose was not only influenced by the similarity of Maserati's Khamsin, but also by the name of a very charming girl – Tasmin – whom Martin knew at the time.

Not only did Lilley want to replace the successful M-Series models, but he wanted to fight for markets which were progressively being abandoned by Triumph and MG. It was not without significance that in 1976 the MGB GT V8 was dropped and it had become clear that the high-performance derivatives of the Triumph TR7 were in danger of cancellation.

By 1977 he had commissioned a freelance engineer-stylist, Oliver Winterbottom, to produce a new design (the designer of the M-Series chassis, Mike Bigland, had long since left TVR), and by the end of that year Winterbottom was devoting all his time to the project. Winterbottom had started his motor industry career at Jaguar as an apprentice, later joined that company's styling division, and had been styling manager at Lotus when the Elite and Eclat models were being shaped in the early Seventies. Ian Jones, also ex-Lotus, designed the chassis and running gear to TVR's requirements. The prototype was on the road in 1978 (TVR then had a separate development factory near Preston), tooling went ahead in 1979 and the first production cars were started in November 1979. Announcement of the fixed-head model came in January 1980, with the drophead and +2 versions being unveiled just in time for showing at the British motor show at the NEC in October 1980. Many more derivatives followed in the next few years.

Although the fixed-head model was announced first, the design of all three was progressed at the same time. However, for all practical purposes it was only desirable to build a single model during most of 1980, as this would not only allow the 100-strong workforce to get thoroughly used to the new

Detail touches in the new two-seater TVR Tasmin Coupe included twin exhaust tail-pipes poking out through body apertures, the use of Ford Capri tail-lamps, the special cast-alloy wheels and the full-width glass panel in the tail, below the normal lift-up hatchback glass door. *(TVR)*

The TVR for the Eighties – the Tasmin Coupe, announced in January 1980. Virtually every part of the car was different from those used in the M-Series models of the Seventies, but the design philosophy of using a multi-tubular backbone chassis-frame, a glass-fibre bodyshell, all-independent suspension and Ford powertrain had been retained. The car was designed for TVR by Oliver Winterbottom, an ex-Jaguar stylist and the person responsible for the shape of the Lotus Elite and Eclat models of the Seventies. The car illustrated is one of the first few Tasmins built, and is the closed two-seater derivative. Subsequently, +2 and Convertible versions, all designed at the same time, were revealed. *(TVR)*

The impressive frontal aspect of the original *Tasmin* Coupe, showing the retracted headlamp pods, the louvred bonnet moulding, which was shared by the Tasmin Convertible but *not* by the +2 derivative, and the neatly styled bonnet bulge necessary to give clearance over the Ford V6 engine. *(TVR)*

design, but would also allow the broadest spectrum of existing TVR customers to be served immediately. Although it was always understood that a three-model range would appear, it was also accepted that they could not all be announced at once.

In its design philosophy and general layout the Tasmin was the same sort of car as the M-Series which it superseded except that the +2 derivative was entirely new to TVR. The basis of the car was a multi-tubular chassis-frame, the bodyshells were built in glassfibre, while competitive service and maintenance costs were ensured by the use of Ford engines and transmissions. There was no direct replacement for the 3000M (which had no lifting tailgate), for customers

now demanded direct access to the storage space behind the seats; the Tasmin fixed-head model, therefore, replaced the Taimar and one Convertible took over from the other.

Like the superseded M-Series, the Tasmin's chassis-frame is the nearest possible equivalent of a spaceframe, and uses the traditional (by TVR standards) 1.5in diameter, 14-gauge steel tubes. It was entirely different in detail, however, and had a longer (7ft 10in) wheelbase than the M-Series frame, while retaining the four-tube backbone type of layout, allied to the use of perimeter tubes to support the floor. The longer wheelbase not only allowed the +2 configuration to be considered, but it also enabled more front seat space to be provided, particularly in terms of the seat back-to-steering

wheel dimension. As usual, there was all-independent coil-spring suspension, but in the Tasmin there were current-model Ford Cortina wishbones at the front, and the rear suspension was all-TVR, with a trailing-arm geometry quite clearly inspired by that of the Lotus Elite/Eclat with which Oliver Winterbottom and Ian Jones were previously linked.

The rack-and-pinion steering came from the Ford Cortina, while the four-wheel Girling disc brakes featured an inboard mounting at the rear, where the calipers were fixed to the Salisbury 4HU final-drive and differential carrier, itself as used on all 3000M/Taimar/Convertible models from March 1977 and shared with such patrician cars as the XJ Jaguars and Aston Martins and Lagondas. The special cast-alloy bolt-on road wheels (there was no wire-wheel option) had a 7in rim width and the 205-section tyres had a squat 60 per cent aspect ratio.

Like British Ford Granadas built since the autumn of 1977, the 1980–81 Reliants and – from the spring of 1981 – certain Ford Capris, the Tasmin used the German Ford V6 engine of 2,792cc. However, it is important to realize not only that

The stubby and distinctive tail-end of the original two-seater TVR Tasmin, revealed in 1980 as the car to replace the M-Series models. *(TVR)*

Lots of straight lines and a walnut-veneer dashboard, with a full range of instruments and controls, in the TVR Tasmin announced in 1980. The facia was standardized for all three initial derivatives. Completely characteristic of all TVRs was the high and wide transmission tunnel, which hid the main longitudinal tubes of the backbone chassis-frame. Electric windows were standard, and their operating switches were housed in the centre console behind the gear-lever. On original cars the handbrake was positioned vertically alongside the gear-lever (almost completely hidden in this picture), but by 1981 it had been repositioned in a horizontal attitude. *(TVR)*

the German V6 was entirely different in detail from the British 'Essex' Ford V6 engine used on the M-Series TVRs, which had different cylinder dimensions and an entirely different cast-iron cylinder block, but that it was considerably more powerful than the old 2,994cc unit. The Tasmin's engine featured Bosch K-Jetronic fuel injection (that of the Granada 2.8i and Capri 2.8 Injection models) and had 160bhp (DIN) at 5,700rpm, compared with the 'Essex' peak output of 138bhp (DIN) at 5,000rpm. The four-speed all-synchromesh gearbox, however, which was as fitted to the equivalent-engined Capri and Granada models, was the same as that of the superseded M-Series TVR. There was no overdrive option – none needed, surely, as the mph/1,000rpm rating was 22.2mph – though the Ford automatic transmission became optional in October 1980, coincident with the release of the Tasmin Convertible and +2 models.

The glassfibre bodyshell was built in two main moulds, joined together at the waist under the decorative strip along the flanks. Barrier impact loads were absorbed with the help of marine plywood diaphragms in certain sections of the

The facia and instrument layout of the TVR Tasmin of 1980, complete with a BL steering column and controls, pedals and various switches. Many of the minor controls, however, were Ford-sourced, which was appropriate as Ford engines and transmissions were also used. *(TVR)*

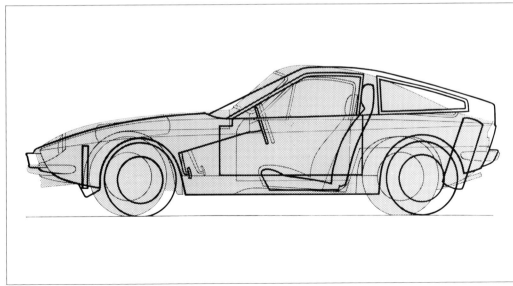

This 'ghosted' comparison shows the difference in profile between the old M-Series TVRs and the Tasmin two-seater of 1980. The Tasmin had a longer wheelbase (7ft 10in, instead of 7ft 6in), a much more steeply raked windscreen and rather more interior space. The tail was higher, which meant that there was more stowage space, and the spare wheel was in the extreme tail, rather than being in the extreme nose, as on M-Series models. *(Autocar)*

The 1980 Tasmin's independent front suspension, of which the general geometry, wishbones, uprights and brakes all came from the latest-model Ford Cortina. Spring and damper rates, of course, were entirely special. The anti-roll bar ran behind the line of the front 'axle', and is not visible in this picture. *(TVR)*

Martin Lilley. The headlamps were hidden away (Lotus and Triumph TR7-style) above the front bumper, while the sharp wedge nose incorporated a combined skirt/air intake, which could be detached for easy repair or replacement after an indiscretion.

Although all three derivatives were based on the same 7ft 10in-wheelbase tubular chassis-frame, there were considerable differences between the bodies, which did not always share the same doors or nose section. To explain this, the original fixed-head coupe – on which, in any case, most of the initial development was done – shall be defined as the 'base' model. The Tasmin Convertible shared the same basic front-end mouldings as the fixed-head car, but had a modified windscreen surround, different door skins – which swept up towards the rear – and an entirely different upper tail-section incorporating a separate stowage area and bootlid.

Detail of the independent rear suspension of the Tasmin, showing the geometry, which was derived from that used by the Lotus Elite and Eclat models of the mid-Seventies. Rear disc brakes are mounted inboard. The components mounted ahead of the semi-trailing suspension arm are the fuel pumps. *(TVR)*

shell, and there were tubular-steel reinforcing beams in the doors to help absorb side impacts. Although special front and rear bumpers were needed before the Tasmin could be exported for sale in North America the rest of the shell incorporated every feature necessary to allow the car to comply with the world's stiffest safety requirement for years ahead.

As usual, it is interesting to see how certain major decorative details had been 'borrowed' from other large-production models to help minimize the investment in a new model. The outside door handles were from the Ford Capri, as were the combined tail-lamp/indicator/reversing-lamp clusters, while the steering column switchgear and steering column lock came from British Leyland.

The style itself, of course, was pure TVR – or, rather, Oliver Winterbottom – with approval and influence by

The rolling chassis of the Tasmin, shared with all three initial derivatives of the design. In general layout, the frame was much as used by M-Series models, but was entirely different in detail. In particular, there was a greatly changed rear suspension, and the V6 Ford engine came from Germany, rather than from the UK. The wheels were new and styled specially for TVR; there was no wire-spoke option. (TVR)

The bare chassis-frame of the 1980 Tasmin, the front-end closest to the camera lens. Though multi-tubular, like the frame of the all previous TVRs, it was entirely new and much more scientific in design. (TVR)

21

Automatic transmission (a three-speed torque converter unit, by Ford) was made optional for the Tasmin from October 1980. It was the very first time that such a transmission had ever been offered on a TVR. Note the revised handbrake position. *(TVR)*

Ready for fitment to the Tasmin is this 2,792cc German Ford V6 engine, complete with some of its fuel-injection equipment and the plenum chamber above the inlet gallery. The cooling fan had a viscous hub and was limited to 2,500rpm. This engine was entirely different, in every way, from the 2,994cc British Ford V6 used in M-Series cars, but was used in the contemporary Ford Granada and Capri 2.8i models, and in smaller and less highly tuned form in other Fords, as well as by Reliant for their Scimitar GTE. *(TVR)*

The +2 not only had a shorter nose, but it had a unique bonnet panel, modified front wheelarches, a different front spoiler and full-length 'running board' skirts between the wheelarches. It also had a longer tail and a modified roof line, not to mention re-arranged floor and petrol tank arrangements, so that the '+2' seating could be inserted behind the normal front seats. Like the Convertible, the +2 had different front and rear bumpers from those fitted to the fixed-head car, though the windscreen and door glasses remained common, as did the front seats, the instrument panel and the facia layout. The rear bumpers also became common. Such a complex, but entirely logical, layout of a model range could only have been achieved at a sensible price by designing all three cars at the same time.

Although the two-seater derivatives had twin interconnected fuel tanks, each of seven gallons, mounted at each side

Overhead shot of the engine bay of the Tasmin, well-filled by the German Ford 2,792cc Ford V6 engine, which developed 160bhp. It featured Bosch K-Jetronic mechanical fuel-injection, the business end of which was tucked away towards the front left of the bay and was identified by the bunched fuel-pipes. In almost every way, this engine was identical with that normally fitted to Ford Granada 2.8i models at the time. *(TVR)*

As with the later M-Series cars, the Tasmin was equipped with a Salisbury 4HU final-drive and differential. This was basically of the same type as used by – among others – Jaguar and Aston Martin for their current models. Like these cars, too, the Tasmin had inboard-mounted disc brakes. *(TVR)*

of the chassis backbone, immediately ahead of the rear suspension, that of the +2 was a single 14-gallon container mounted above the line of the rear wheels; this move was necessary to allow the '+2' seating to be installed without lengthening the wheelbase. The fixed-head and the +2 models both had large, full-width, glass hatchbacks, hinged at the front in the roof, and these gave easy access to the spare wheel, tucked vertically in the tail in time-honoured Grantura fashion. A feature of the Convertible model was that it could be used with the hood and its supports completely folded away, or with a hefty roll-over bar – called a 'rear header' in TVR publicity literature – erected.

For the Tasmin, a new sequence of Chassis Numbers was chosen. The last M-Series (a Convertible Turbo) was 4970FM, with no prefix. The first production Tasmin was given the Chassis Number FH5001FI – where FH stands for

A feature of the Tasmin Convertible was that the stout roll-over bar could be folded back to the position shown, so as to offer true open-air motoring in ideal conditions. Unlike the obsolete M-Series Convertible, or 3000S, the Tasmin Convertible had wind-down window glasses, which are fully retracted in this pose. *(TVR)*

Fixed Head and FI for Fuel Injection. Later in the sequence, as the Appendices make clear, a DH prefix was adopted for the Drophead, or Convertible Tasmin, while the advent of the +2 model was signalled by the addition of a number '2' as the final suffix to the Chassis Number.

Just six Tasmins (all fixed-head models) were started in 1979, so the first 1980 number was FH5007. By the end of 1980, a total of 148 Tasmins of all types had been started, and the first 1981 number to be started was FH5148F12 – a +2 model. Then, in the spring of 1981, after 18 months' production, the original two-seater fixed-head bodyshell was discontinued, and in its place the Series 2 Coupe was given a two-seater derivative of the short-nose/long-tail +2 bodyshell, which meant that it had the different bonnet and the front spoiler and was given the 'running board' skirts. Inside the

car, however, the twin fuel-tank installation was retained and a new glassfibre boot-floor moulding was grafted in to provide more than 16cu ft of carrying capacity. The Convertible bodyshell, however, was not changed. The last Series 1 two-seater fixed-head Tasmin was FH5196FI, started in March 1981, while the first Series 2 version was FH5211FIT, started in April. That chassis suffix (FIT, where the T stood for Series 2), was soon altered, and from June 1981 Series 2 fixed-heads have numbers like 2FH5232FI. It is worth noting that the 200th Tasmin was built in April 1981.

New models – and new management
In the next 12 months there would be big changes at Blackpool, for not only were several new models initiated or

The '+2' seating of the Tasmin +2 Coupe, showing that with the front seats in their fully-back position there was no legroom at all. Finding space for these occasional rear seats meant moving the two fuel tanks (normally on the floor of the chassis, behind the seats of the two-seaters) and replacing them by a single 14-gallon (Imperial) tank mounted above the line of the rear suspension and final-drive unit. *(TVR)*

Much ingenuity went into arranging for a +2 version of the Tasmin Coupe to be possible without ruining the lines. The car was immediately recognizable at first by the different front spoiler and by the moulded 'runningboards' under the doors, but it should also be noted that the nose ahead of the front wheels was shorter than on other Tasmins, that there was an entirely different bonnet moulding without louvres, and that the detail shaping of the rear quarters was also subtly changed. Compared with the original two-seater Coupe Tasmin, the +2 version was 3in longer overall. The doors, incidentally, were the same as those of the two-seater Tasmin. This bodyshell was also adopted for the two-seater Tasmin Coupe in May 1981. *(TVR)*

A detail of the +2 Coupe, showing the radio loudspeaker position, the inertia-reel safety belt pivot, and the almost complete lack of legroom in the back. *(TVR)*

announced, but the business also changed hands. As 1981 progressed, sales showed no signs of picking up again to the 1979 (pre-Tasmin) levels. For instance, 308 cars had been sold in 1979, but only 144 in 1980.

Profitability suffered badly, and for a time the prospects for TVR looked grim. Investment in the new Tasmin was not paying off, and with the car not yet 'federalized', the potentially lucrative US market was temporarily out of reach.

At this point, an enthusiastic Tasmin owner, Peter Wheeler – who had bought a very early example, FH5014FI, in 1980 – came on to the scene and bought control from Martin Lilley at the end of 1981. But TVR was by no means a new scene to him: "Initially I bought a Taimar Turbo, had it serviced here in Blackpool, and gradually came to know people and be drawn into the company's activities. It was Stewart Halstead who actually got me involved, and I became a major shareholder when I saw that there were certain problems which I could help to solve."

Peter Wheeler was a graduate chemical engineer who had started his first business in 1972 with a capital of £200. He then made his fortune supplying specialist equipment to the booming North Sea oil industry. When he took control at TVR, less than 10 years later, he was 38 years old. He became TVR's Chairman, and appointed Stewart Halstead as Managing Director.

As Stewart told me in the early Eighties: "Soon after Peter took over, we established a five-year plan, and one of my first priorities was to improve the build quality and our own manufacturing content even further. The Tasmin chassis is excellent, and we wouldn't want to replace it yet, not for several years. It is a very versatile frame."

That five-year plan, and the versatility of the chassis design, was gradually unveiled in the years which followed.

The 2-litre Tasmin

No four-cylinder-engined TVR had been on offer since 1977, when the last of the 1600Ms was delivered, but in October 1981 the Tasmin 200 came along to fill that gap. TVR's publicity material noted the discontinuation of the Triumph TR7, and suggested that the new model could take over from it!

Development of this model had been quick and easy, for the 200 was effectively a Tasmin with an engine/gearbox transplant; in place of the Ford-Cologne powertrain there was a 101bhp 1,993cc Ford 'Pinto' (officially 'T88') overhead-cam four-cylinder engine and four-speed gearbox, as normally found in the Capri 2000 and Cortina 2000 models. Compared with the 2.8-litre models, the performance was somewhat reduced, though TVR claimed a top speed of 115mph, with a 0–60mph acceleration in 9 seconds.

The 2-litre engine was available for the Tasmin in two-seater Coupe or Convertible form, but was never offered with the '+2' seating arrangement, and the only significant chassis change was the fitment of reduced-section tyres on 6in wheel rims. To get the price down to an astonishingly low £9,885 for the Convertible, £9,985 for the Coupe, a few of the original Tasmin's 'frills' were deleted – there were no electric window lifts or radio/cassette player – but the rolling chassis

This three-quarter-rear view of the 1981-model Tasmin Convertible shows the instantly recognizable body style, the differently-shaped doors, the neatly folded hood and bracing roll-over bar and the separate boot compartment access. The incorporation of the 'Tasmin' name into the body side flash is a particularly neat touch. *(TVR)*

The Series 2 Tasmin two-seater Coupe used the long-tail +2 bodyshell, but kept its own arrangement of twin fuel tanks, one on each side of the chassis backbone, behind the seats, and had a long flat loading area; the carrying capacity was increased to more than 16 cubic feet. From this view, the way to identify a Series 2 two-seater from the +2 is by the location of the fuel tank filler caps; on the two-seater they are mounted well forward, near the door shut lines, whereas on the +2 they are located further back, above and behind the rear wheelarches. *(TVR)*

was the same as before.

The rationale behind the 200 was Martin Lilley's way of bringing Tasmin prices back to the level of the 1979 Taimar, and it was hoped that the sub-£10,000 price would make it an attractive 'businessman's express' as well. However, although it was well received, it did not sell as well as had been hoped, but as the 200 made very little money for TVR in any case, this may have been fortunate. Peter Wheeler was actually quite irritated by the 200's sales rate, saying that it was "an amazing bargain", but Stewart Halstead was much more attracted to the idea of selling more large-engine TVRs to export markets, particularly North America. In the end,

only 61 cars (16 Coupes and 45 Convertibles) were built, the last of all being produced in September 1984.

Tasmin Turbo

The story of this intriguing project is told in more detail in Chapter 8, but at this stage it is worth recalling that it was first schemed out in 1980, the first prototype (a Convertible) was built in 1981, and the Coupe was shown at the British motor show at the NEC in October 1982. In 1981, Martin Lilley was quoted as stating: "Demand exists here and abroad for an out-and-out powerhouse that sacrifices nothing in pursuit of excellent road manners and a blistering performance", and

For the Tasmin 200 model, TVR used the Ford Pinto (T88) 2-litre overhead cam engine. This fitted easily into a space which readily accepted bulkier engines (such as the Rover V8 unit). With only a single downdraught carburettor, and 101bhp, this was hardly an inspiring power unit – perhaps this explains why only 61 such cars were ever sold. *(TVR)*

The Series 2 Tasmin became the 280i in 1983, and in this form (note the very large shock-absorbing bumpers) it was also put on sale in North America. *(TVR)*

The 1986-model 'federal' 280i Convertible featured these neatly swept door mirrors, and had much neater bumper outlines than the original US-market car. *(TVR)*

Peter Wheeler took control of TVR in the early Eighties. Except for the original concept of the Tasmin family, he takes credit for the development of all TVRs of the Eighties and Nineties. *(TVR)*

even though management control had changed by that time, the Tasmin Turbo was revealed in prototype form a year later. Peter Wheeler, however, was not altogether convinced that this was the right sort of ultra-high-performance car he wanted TVR to be building in the mid-Eighties.

Developments with the Ford V6-engined cars
A great deal of work was done to the design of the Tasmin family of cars in the Eighties, and although most changes were made to all the cars, for the moment attention must be drawn to those of the Ford V6-engined models. It is interesting

to note, incidentally, that in 1980, the first year of production, Tasmins were sold to personalities like Tony Jacklin, Peter Wheeler and Stuart Hall, while later cars went to footballer Gary Birtles, Victor Gauntlett – later Chairman of Aston Martin – and *Fast Lane* magazine. The first Tasmin (Chassis No FH5005FI) was later re-registered ECW 440W; both were eventually sold off – and are perhaps still out there somewhere.

The original cars used TVR wheels, then Momo cast-alloy road wheels were adopted, but during 1982 some cars were fitted with the 'spider's web' pattern of cast-alloy wheel from BHS, which was soon standardized. It was around this period that the Tasmin 200 was equipped with twin fuel tanks. From October 1982, when Ford released all-synchromesh five-speed gearboxes for their cars, these were made optional – but never standard – on the Tasmin range.

The most important development of 1983 was that TVR regained a foothold in the US market with the de-toxed 2.8-litre Tasmin in either Convertible or – much more rarely – Coupe form. The arduous certification work was shared between TVR themselves and (for engine work and other details) TUV in Germany. Even though a three-way catalyst was required for the exhaust emissions to meet regulations, peak power was still 145bhp (as against the European car's 160bhp, which was in any case de-rated to 150bhp at about that time). A four-speed gearbox was still standard, and the US cars weighed about 300lb more than the European types.

At first, the US market was serviced by the Canadian importer, who had been loyal to TVR for 15 years, and whose brochures wisely advised the enthusiast to 'Experience the rarity of TVR', for it was some time before supplies grew significantly. Before the end of the year, however, it was decided to service the United States directly, and Stewart Halstead eventually set up TVR of America Inc, headed by David Beesley, who had been President of Volvo-USA for the previous two decades. The operation was originally based at Jacksonville, Florida, but it later moved to Connecticut and at one time was handling as much as 60 per cent of total TVR production.

It was the success of the export drive, not only to the USA, but to territories like Singapore and the Middle East, which then led TVR to consider rationalizing the product line. During 1984, as already stated, the slow-selling 2-litre model was phased out, and at the same time the decision was taken to drop the +2 Coupe.

As Stewart Halstead admitted: "We introduced the +2 after listening to dealers and customers. But with the existing chassis and wheelbase we really couldn't provide much space for back seats, and I think customers really expected too much."

The fact was that with the front seats in their rearmost position on the slides, there was no '+2' legroom at all, so all that was left was a pair of expensively trimmed luggage-carrying areas. Incidentally, Murphy's Law applied to the decision to drop the +2 models; when it was announced in 1984, three customers hurried to order cars – a 350i and two 280i models! The last +2 was built in September 1985.

During the autumn of 1984, it was decided to phase out the name 'Tasmin' completely in Europe (although most TVR enthusiasts continue to quote it as the family name for the Eighties' TVRs). The decision was influenced partly because there were several different engine sizes to be advertised – and more were planned – and partly because in a subtle way the Wheeler-Halstead team wanted to distance itself from the previous management and its products. Accordingly, and

TVR's motor show stands attracted some distinguished visitors in the early Eighties. Here, TVR's owner, Martin Lilley, demonstrates the soft-top folding system of the Tasmin to HRH Prince Michael of Kent. *(TVR)*

without fuss, the Tasmin 2.8-litre became the 280i, with no more than a few badging and brochure changes to note the junction. The name was retained on US-market cars until October 1985.

1985 and 1986 – the Series 2 models

Once the Rover-engined 390SE had been launched (see Chapter 3), there was time to consider changes and improvements to the other cars in the range. From the autumn of 1984 (and still retaining the 'Tasmin' name for another season), the US-specification 280i became 'Series 1½', which was an official title used only inside the TVR factory. There were no important mechanical changes, but visual alteration included the use of different bumpers, a modified front air dam and Rover SD1-style tail-lamps. All of these cars had full air conditioning – which does *not* mean that the roof could be retracted! – metallic paintwork and hide seats.

Then, in the summer of 1985, the US-specification 280i Convertible also officially became Series 2, with the same series of visual changes as for the Rover-engined 350i, and from early 1986 the UK-market car followed suit, all of which helped to reduce the number of different bodyshells which TVR had to produce. These external changes, incidentally, were made only to the Convertibles, for very few Coupes were being built by this time, and existing body styles were retained for these orders.

By the end of 1985, all cars, whether Rover-engined or not, were being fitted with Rover radiators (the Ford-engined car had previously used a different radiator), but soon after this there was an important change to the TVR chassis when a

This has to be a weekend shot – the shop floor deserted, and only a few Tasmin chassis are in evidence. No records remain, but I date this picture in the winter of 1979/80, just when the Tasmin family was starting to be built at Bristol Avenue. The Tasmin's chassis jig is in the foreground. *(TVR)*

This overhead study of a V6-engined Tasmin engine bay shows that there was plenty of space up front, even with an air conditioning pump in place – until, that is, the radiators were slotted into place. (TVR)

new type of rear suspension was specified.

Developed on the latest racing car (see Chapter 8), this featured the use of a fully triangulated lower wishbone, with two pick-up points to a new upright instead of the simpler, forward-mounted trailing-arm and lower-link arrangement of the earlier models. This not only eliminated any small amounts of torque steer which could previously be induced, but allowed fine adjustment of the suspension geometry.

The first customer car to have the rear suspension was DH169RI, built in November 1985, the next was DH222RI,

built in January 1986, (both these being 350is) and after a batch had been sent to Germany in April 1986 it was standardized on all cars.

In the meantime, all manner of important, though mainly 'invisible', improvements were being made to the cars. New features of the US-specification 280i Convertible, for instance, included the use of Silentbloc bush mountings between chassis-frame and bodyshell, a fully adjustable steering column (height, reach and tilt), an air-blending heating-and-ventilation system, and the use of a small-diameter Space-

By 1986 the Ford-engined 280i models were nearing the end of their career. They had been updated to Series 2 styling specification, which included skirts under the rear bumper; the twin exhaust outlets remained. Mass exports of Convertibles to the USA ended in 1986, and the arrival of the new S in 1987 marked the end of the 280i Convertible. *(TVR)*

saver tyre. It would be quite impossible to detail the number of improvements made to the trim, instruments, fittings and decoration in recent years – but regular TVR customers would certainly notice the changes. The bonnet panel, for instance, has been changed several times, on several models, to improve not only the looks, but the engine bay ventilation through-flow.

After 1986 the 280i model gradually took a back seat at TVR. When Peter Wheeler took over complete control in 1987 by buying Managing Director Stewart Halstead's share of the business, he and his staff became almost totally bound up in the launch of the new 'retro' S model, in the big Rover-engined versions of the 280i chassis, and in developing the 420SEAC model.

The production figures tell their own story. In 1986 a total of 149 280i cars – almost all of which were shipped to the USA – were produced. Immediately after this TVR pulled out of that market for reasons which Wheeler made crystal clear in later years: "We used to be highly dependent on the export market. We've sold, I would guess, to every country in the world bar none in the past...and we find long-term relationships with these importers extremely difficult to maintain. I think the main reason is our lack of management overhead to actually look after them.

"In the mid-Eighties 70 per cent of our production went to the States, and that's been easily my biggest crisis – when we fell out with the importer for not paying for some cars and not looking after them, and having a lot of hassle.

"We are very wary of markets other than the UK whereby there seems to be a rush of orders...".

He is now very careful *not* to be dependent on exports, and he swears that he will never sell a TVR to America again from his factory.

This explains why 280i production dropped like a stone in 1987, to a mere 35 cars (four of them being fixed-head Coupes). The last five 280is, all Convertibles, were produced early in 1988. By that time TVR enthusiasts had fallen in love with the latest Ford V6-engined car, the much cheaper S roadster.

Not that this signalled the end of the original Tasmin-style chassis, for in 1983 the first of the Rover V8-engined versions, named 350i, had been introduced. This was a move of great significance, for cars of this basic type were produced from 1983 to 1991. The evolution of the layout deserves a complete chapter of its own.

CHAPTER 3

Rover power for the mid-Eighties

350i, 390SE and derivatives from 1983

Once the Tasmin had gone on sale in 1980, and TVR production had recovered from the major upheaval caused by clearing out everything to do with the old M-Type/Taimar models, Martin Lilley and Stewart Halstead set about expanding the range of options. Because both were real sportscar enthusiasts, it was almost inevitable that they would consider making more powerful versions.

But which engine should be used? As is now known, TVR eventually chose the ubiquitous Rover V8, but before this decision was made, in 1981 and 1982, work began on a turbocharged version of the 2.8-litre Ford V6 engine which was already being used in the Tasmin family. The result was the development of the Tasmin Turbo.

The story of this intriguing project is told in more detail in Chapter 8, but at this stage it is worth recalling the timetable at Blackpool. The Turbo's design was first schemed out in 1980, the first prototype (a convertible) was built in 1981, and the second car – a hatchback coupe, visually based on the standard Tasmin style – was shown at the British motor show at the NEC in October 1982.

In 1981 Martin Lilley had been quoted as saying: "Demand exists here and abroad for an out-and-out powerhouse that sacrifices nothing in pursuit of excellent road manners and a blistering performance", and even though management control had changed by that time, the Tasmin Turbo was revealed in prototype form a year later.

TVR's new proprietor, Peter Wheeler, was not altogether convinced that this was precisely the correct sort of ultra-high-performance car he wanted TVR to be building in the mid-Eighties. He wanted to produce high performance from a deep-breathing, torquey and normally-aspirated engine instead of one which relied on turbocharging. The result was that after only two prototypes had been built, the Tasmin Turbo project was scrapped, and all the knowledge gained went into a very different type of TVR.

350i – the mighty Rover V8-engined TVR

Although TVR's biggest project in 1983 was reopening the US market with the 2.8-litre-engined cars, there were good reasons for producing a new, larger-engined, super-TVR as well. There was the fact that the normally-aspirated Ford 2.8-litre engine was at the limit of its development, also that in some potentially profitable export markets the name 'Ford' was politically unacceptable.

Peter Wheeler and Stewart Halstead therefore looked around for an alternative source of supply, and like several other independent manufacturers, before and since, they decided that the light-alloy Rover V8 engine was ideal. Although it was physically quite large – necessitating changes to the tubular chassis-frame to accept it – it was a very simple, torquey unit; in its latest Lucas-injected 'Vitesse' form it produced 190bhp, and no less than 220lb.ft of torque at 4,000rpm, and could be backed by the robust five-speed all-synchromesh transmission which was also found in cars as diverse as the Jaguar XJ6, the – obsolete – Triumph TR7/TR8 and the Morgan Plus 8.

The introduction of the new Rover V8-engined car also signalled TVR's intention to drop the 'Tasmin' name in due

The Eighties' management team, enjoying themselves at a race-car testing day. Peter Wheeler (with moustache) became TVR's owner in 1981 while Stewart Halstead was then Managing Director. *(TVR)*

course, for they liked to refer to it by the simple designation '350i' – denoting 3.5-litre engine, with fuel injection. It was also the point at which several important chassis changes were made.

Ex-Formula 1 driver John Miles, when describing the new car in *Autocar* of August 27, 1983, commented: "Let no man say that British car manufacturers cannot respond quickly to a demand. At the motor show last year, TVR were still thinking exclusively of Ford power for their cars – including a turbocharged Ford V6 for their new flagship.

"But an inquiry from an Arab state – where the name of Ford has almost as much appeal as Tournedos Rossini to a vegetarian – produced a lightning rethink that, with hindsight, may have opened new routes of progression for the Blackpool concern.

"The point is, the TVR 350i not only goes much better than its Ford V6, 160bhp fuel-injected-engine sisters, but it also has – not before time – a much improved chassis whose handling and ride conform far more to the high-performance car ideal. In truth, the TVR Tasmin 350i is a completely

different motor car." (The 'Tasmin' name was not yet dead!)

Under the skin, in fact, the chassis-frame was widened by 1.5 inches around the engine bay, but there were major changes to the front suspension. On the original 2.8-litre Tasmins this had been criticized as being too soft, and there had been severe steering kickback over potholes.

To rectify these problems, the new chief development engineer, John Box, modified the Ford Cortina-based layout considerably. The original design had used a lower tie-bar, operating in compression to absorb longitudinal forces, and in place of this he specified a forward-facing bar operating in tension. At the same time he reduced this bar's inward-pointing angle to reduce its compliance and therefore some of the gyroscopic forces which helped generate steering kick. The anti-roll bar was also relocated, ahead of the line of the suspension, and almost doubled in diameter from 0.625 to 1.125in, while front spring rates were increased by 17 per cent.

There was a new large Rover radiator up front, and although the first cars were fitted with power-sapping Land Rover V8-style cast exhaust manifolds, TVR soon developed

The 350i model (which was briefly badged 'Tasmin' as well) was announced in 1983, and used a 190bhp Rover Vitesse V8 engine. Note the front spoiler (different from that of the current 280i, and including extra driving lamps as standard). *(TVR)*

A study in tails. The original Tasmin 350i of 1983, with a single exhaust tail-pipe, was fitted with Rover-type tail-lamp clusters (left), while the 1985–86 variety (right) had twin exhaust tailpipes, and Renault Fuego-type tail-lamps. *(TVR)*

The bulky, but lightweight, Rover V8 engine was a snug fit in the engine bay, which had been originally designed around the smaller Ford V6 unit. *(TVR)*

fabricated tubular manifolds instead, which allowed a few more bhp to be liberated; these were fitted from DH 5870RI. A few cars were built with the same automatic transmission as was being used in Rover cars of the period.

Although the original 350i was announced only as a Convertible, in August 1983, the first car had been built in March and the first Coupe version in May, while the first +2 model would follow in September 1983. By the end of the calendar year, 65 Rover-engined cars had been produced, and all three body types became officially available from the beginning of 1984.

Even though it could not be sold in the USA, the 350i was

a great new TVR development, as the sales figures soon testified; production continued to rise until, by 1986, the Rover V8-engined cars had all but taken over completely at Blackpool. The 350i, of course, was a very fast car – magazine tests quoted a top speed of around 136mph – but it could also be surprisingly economical; because it was no heavier than the Ford V6-engined car, it was quite easy for up to 22mpg to be recorded, even while the driver was enjoying the colossal acceleration and much improved handling.

Sales trends at TVR had been changing steadily since 1981, but from the day the 350i went 'on stream' in Blackpool, these intensified. Not only did more orders come in for V8-engined cars, but even more Convertibles were sold. In 1983, for instance, 142 cars (of 204 in all) were Convertibles – but in 1984 there were 262 out of 335 and the proportion was to increase still further in the next two years.

390SE Convertible – TVR's mid-Eighties Supercar

In October 1984, TVR showed that their performance ambitions had no limits. The 350i might, indeed, be a very fast car, but Wheeler and Halstead thought they could do even better. On a strictly limited-production basis, and originally with the help of Rover engine specialist Andy Rouse, they decided to produce the ferociously fast and powerful 390SE Convertible – and even that wasn't the ultimate stretch of this amazing sportscar design.

As TVR's own press release of October 15, 1984 stated: "A new generation of high-performance motoring is announced today in the UK... Top speed of over 150mph with blistering acceleration throughout the range must surely make it one of the quickest production convertible sportscars available in the UK... TVR's Chairman, Peter Wheeler, intends to return the sports car to those days of high-performance motoring that fuel crises and ever increasing legislation have almost wiped out...". In other words, it was meant to be an indulgence for well-off sportscar enthusiasts – but it was firmly intended to be a profitable project for TVR as well. In every way it was going to be a better and faster car than the stillborn Tasmin Turbo.

Visually, the new 390SE was much like every other current TVR Convertible except that it had a much deeper front spoiler – which incorporated brake-cooling ducts – along with an under-tail aerofoil section, both of which were used to trim the aerodynamics. The '390SE' badging on the tail, front spoiler and flanks told 'the other fellow' about the car which had just passed him with such verve.

The secret of the 390SE, and the reason for its title, was that the Rover V8 engine had been enlarged to 3,905cc – by a cylinder bore increase – and totally rebuilt and redeveloped by Andy Rouse's race-preparation business. In a process which encompassed a special crankshaft, Cosworth pistons, gas-flowed cylinder heads, high-lift camshaft profiles, larger valves and stronger valve gear, Rouse produced an engine with no less than 275bhp at 5,500rpm.

This was backed by a stronger clutch, a Torsen gear-type limited-slip differential, 15in wheels and 225-section VR-rated Yokohama tyres, while there were four-pot brake calipers on ventilated front disc brakes. All in all, it was an astonishing 'personalization' of an already outstanding design, but once again John Miles of *Autocar* shall be left to sum up events so well: "The nice memories are of the way it would lope along at unmentionable speeds on a whisker of throttle, its animal get-up-and-go, the grip and wonderfully predictable medium-speed handling. You could say that happiness is £19,700, a deserted roundabout, and a 390SE to play with...".

That sum, by the way, was made up of the full price of £15,540 for a 350i Convertible and £4,160 for the work done to convert it into a 390SE Convertible; the point is that the 390SE was a conversion, not a completely built model in its own right.

Because of its high price, the considerable hand-work which went into the rebuilding of the engine, back axle, brakes and bodywork, and its very specialized nature, only a limited number of 390SEs could be made. In fact, only five cars were built in 1984 and a further 13 followed in 1985. In the summer of 1986, by which time a further 15 cars had been produced, the modification of the engines had been taken over by TVR itself, and even at a UK total price of £20,937 there was no slackening of demand.

Some people, of course, are never satisfied, and have the money available to make a car like the 390SE even more special. This explains why a number of 390SEs were produced with the long-stroke 4,228cc Rover V8 engine which was being prepared for the forthcoming 420SEAC model, and peak power was further increased to 300bhp; the first of these cars was built in March 1985.

1985 and 1986 – the Series 2 models

In the spring of 1985, the 350i Convertible progressed to Series 2 specification – the first such car was Chassis No DH5980RI, but series production began in April 1985 with the new VIN number identification – at which point there was subtle reshaping of the front end of the car to make it

By 1986, the 280i/350i/390SE cars were being fitted with VDO instruments, though the general layout was much as it had been throughout the Tasmin family's life. *(TVR)*

Compared with other cars of this family, the 1984–85 390SE Convertible had a deeper and more functional front spoiler, and there was a different bonnet panel, including a unique air intake on the left side. *(TVR)*

more rounded, while new bumpers, airdam and sill extensions, as already found on the 'Series 1½' US-specification 280i, were all standardized. These changes, along with yet another upgrading of the instruments and cockpit fittings – this was almost an annual occurrence at TVR! – and standardization of central door locking and electric bootlid release, made a great car even better.

The different type of wishbone rear suspension, featuring a sturdier lower wishbone and forward-facing radius arms, was phased in on the 350i/390SE models during 1986, and in spite of the attention focused on the trio of new cars shown later that year – 420SEAC, S and 420 Sports Saloon – what was now becoming thought of as the 'traditional' style of TVR continued selling well.

TVR never sold the Rover V8-engined cars to the US market, so when sales of Ford V6-engined cars to that market died away rapidly (as described in Chapter 2), TVR was able to take up some of the slack by producing more V8-engined cars for Britain and a few other export territories.

Production of the 350i continued on until August 1990, while further developments of the design – especially the mighty 450SE – were built until October 1991. In the final years there were few obvious changes to the style, or to the basic engineering, though many minor but significant improvements were made.

Between 1986 and 1991 the TVR business was transformed, for Peter Wheeler took sole control in 1987, the first of the new 'rounded' TVRs (the Tuscan) appeared in 1988, this being followed by the curvaceous Griffith of 1990. Even so there was great continuity around the Tasmin/280i/350i family, for in that time the Rover-engined car was made in two styles – Convertible and Coupe – with five different Rover-based engines: 350i, 390SE, 400SE, 420SE and 450SE. It was a busy, not to say confusing, period of TVR's history. It is hoped that the following notes will explain the sequence of events:

The 1986-style rear suspension, first developed on the factory-sponsored race cars, featured a sturdy lower wishbone and radius arms. *(TVR)*

Mid-1986: 350i Convertible and 350i Coupe available. 390SE available as an 'option package'. For favoured customers, a '420SE' package was also available in 1986.

350i models had the 3,528cc engine
390SE models had the 3,905cc engine
420SE models had the 4,228cc engine

In 1984 *Autocar* had described the 3.9-litre-engined car as 'the first real blood and guts sports car to come from this side of the Channel in ages', but the same team of testers found the 390SE of 1987 to be a different animal. This time the impression was of 'a sort of halfway house between the mainline 350i and the Rambo-esque 420SEAC'. Certainly the performance – with a 0–100mph sprint taking only 15.4sec, and with a top speed of 143mph – was exhilarating by any standards, and the quality of manufacture, allied to the subtly of the looks, seemed to improving all the time.

October 1988: Range reshuffled. 350i now joined by 400SE and 450SE. Style and equipment improvements included an integrated front bumper/airdam/side skirt style, along with new headlamps in redesigned pods.

350i models retained the 3,528cc engine
400SE models had a 3,948cc engine
450SE models had a 4,441cc engine

Both the enlarged engines had a 94mm (instead of a 93.5mm) cylinder bore, the 4,441cc engine also having a longer 80mm (instead of 71.12mm) stroke.

During the next three years, sales of what was now an old-style range gradually faded away – 245 cars were built in 1989, 128 followed in 1990 and the last 44 in 1991. Cut-off dates were as follows:

By the time V8-engined Tasmin-family cars went on sale, the chassis' front suspension had been modified to include this forward-facing tie-bar operating in tension below the forward-positioned anti-roll bar. *(TVR)*

August 1990: The last 350i was built.
December 1990: The last 450SE was built.
October 1991: The last 400SE was built.

If Martin Lilley, Stewart Halstead and Peter Wheeler had ever taken the time to look back, they would have seen that what I choose to call the 'Tasmin family' had been in production at Blackpool for almost 12 years, and that engines as diverse as the 101bhp 2-litre Ford and the 324bhp 4.4-litre Rover (in 450SEAC form) had been used. Most important of all, the use of this versatile chassis had led to the sale of more than 2,600 cars.

To improve on this, TVR would need to develop an altogether outstanding new car. By looking back *and* looking forward, the team did just that – and the result was the S Roadster, which brought TVR back towards its roots of the Sixties.

This is probably the first time a Rover V8 engine was offered up to the Tasmin chassis. Note the cast exhaust manifolds – and the crowbar in the engineer's hands! TVR abandoned the turbo-charged V6 concept early in 1983, choosing to use the 3.5-litre normally-aspirated Rover engine instead. Derivatives of that engine were still in use at TVR a decade later. *(TVR)*

At one time in the early Eighties TVR dabbled with the idea of approving a supercharged (not turbocharged) Rover installation. The so-called 350SX remained as a one-off prototype, was fitted with an engine modified by Dave Haughin and Dennis Priddel, and had a Sprintex super-charger. The claimed peak horsepower was 260bhp, but TVR later achieved a lot more than this by enlarging the normally-aspirated engine to 4.5 litres. *(TVR)*

The Rover V8 engine is a bulky unit – sizes range from 3.5 litres to a full 5 litres in normally-aspirated form – but all the main castings are in aluminium alloy. Note how much of the length is taken up by auxiliary drives at the front of the cylinder block. *(TVR)*

Stewart Halstead (left) discussing the latest TVR products at an Eighties motor show with HRH the Duke of Kent. *(TVR)*

A mystery picture! The car is a 350i, TVR's own demonstrator model, and the personality on the platform is actor Roy Kinnear – but what is going on? *(TVR)*

Towards the end of its life, the Convertible was beginning to look angular, and the swooping curves of the Griffith finally killed it off. Between 1988 and 1991, however, no fewer than 242 400SE models were produced. *(TVR)*

The 390SE, here seen in Series 2 guise, was a very limited-edition model. The engine produced no less than 275bhp, giving the car a 150mph top speed. The split-rim wheels were standard on this model. *(TVR)*

The most powerful of the long-running Tasmin-family Convertible series was the 450SE, of which just 35 were made in 1989 and 1990. The Rover-derived engine was enlarged to 4,441cc and produced a monstrous 320bhp. No wonder not many customers thought they could cope with it! *(TVR)*

When the 400SE's headlamps were flipped up, the smooth lines of the body style were lost, and because of the extra drag, the top speed was significantly reduced. *(TVR)*

There was space, but little to spare, for the 90-degree Rover V8 engine to be slotted into the modified Tasmin chassis. Even more powerful versions of this 1983 development were built at TVR until 1991. *(TVR)*

A star shines – or is that too trite? Whatever, this is a striking study of the 350i in the dusk, foglamps ablaze... *(TVR)*

CHAPTER 4

TVR S

1986 – The two-seater roadster reborn

Throughout the Eighties TVR had continued to surprise the pundits by launching a flood of new models, few of which had been expected, forecast or leaked in advance. Peter Wheeler, who liked good jokes, especially if he was making them, was delighted by this.

Critics sometimes lashed him, in print, either for announcing a new car before he was ready to put it on sale, or for announcing a new model which was eventually cancelled before sales had even begun, but he rarely reacted. TVR, after all, was *his* company, and if he got the strategy wrong it was his bank account alone which would suffer. Anyway, he might have said – and the evidence backed this up – that he *loved* cars, *loved* inspiring new models, and would continue doing just that if his company could afford it.

In the mid-Eighties, the most unexpected new model of all was the S Convertible, which came together, as a project, in a rush in the summer of 1986, and which was previewed at the NEC motor show before it was ready to be sold. It was vital to TVR's future because it pushed the company back into a price bracket which it had long abandoned and it was the first model to move away from an established chassis design since the Tasmin had appeared, nearly seven years earlier. Once on the market, and selling at a remarkably low price, it transformed TVR's fortunes. Between 1986, when it was previewed, and 1988, the first full year of S-series build, TVR's annual production leapt from 396 to 701.

Yet even as late as September 1986, with the motor show only four weeks away, TVR's spokesman, Noel Palmer, admitted that a final choice of engine – between the 2.8-litre Ford V6, the fuel-injected 2-litre M16 four-cylinder unit from Austin-Morris, or the 2.2-litre Peugeot fuel-injected engine – had yet to be made; perhaps Noel was being a touch political, rather economical with the truth, for when I saw the partly finished prototype at that time it already had a Ford V6 engine installed.

When the public first saw it in Birmingham, at first glance it looked just like the old 3000S Convertible of 1978 and 1979! Some of the body lines, in fact, *were* the same, but under the skin, and in many other important details, it was a completely new concept.

The car's secret lay not in its appeal to instant nostalgia and its throwback to Seventies' TVR looks, but in its very attractive price. TVR prices had risen considerably since 1979, and when the Tasmin-based 280i Convertible was dropped from the British market in the autumn of 1986 it was priced at £15,200. Because the new-type S Convertible was provisionally priced at £12,995 in October 1986, this compared very well with the 1986 350i Convertible price of £17,865. Quite suddenly, a new TVR was appealing to a different, somewhat wider, market.

At the time, production of the S Convertible was not yet ready to begin, but there was such a startling response at the NEC motor show that it looked as if sales would begin early in 1987.

Although the new S was like other modern TVRs in that it had a separate tubular chassis and all-independent suspension, its chassis design was completely new, and incorporated a semi-trailing-link rear end. The fuel-injected V6 engine and

A famous style was effectively reborn in 1986, when the S Sports car was revealed. Although this had many features of the well-loved 3000S Convertible of 1978–79, there was a completely new chassis design, the 280i running gear, a new windscreen, and many other details. The *real* attraction of this car, at the time, was its very competitive price tag – only £12,995. *(TVR)*

The chassis of the S was totally different from that of the Tasmin-family cars. In particular, it featured a semi-trailing rear suspension system, and the first-generation cars also had drum rear brakes. *(TVR)*

five-speed gearbox were those of the existing 280i models, though instead of the four-disc brake system there was a disc front/drum rear installation. With 150bhp on tap, TVR claimed a top speed of 135mph.

The body style, though superficially familiar, was really very different from that of the old-style 3000S. The *basic* lines and some of the proportions had been retained, though the air scoop in the bonnet top was new, as were the positions of the side/indicator lamps, the wheelarch profiles, the windscreen frame and many other details. The whole car was several inches wider than the 1978–79 version, and in the reborn model there were to be wind-up door windows. Not only that, but the Eighties-style Tasmin Convertible type of fold-down roll bar was also to be incorporated.

The next few years promised to be extremely exciting for the little Blackpool concern, and the sales figures proved, without question, that the dodgy days of 1981 and 1982 were

The prototype S Convertible, as unveiled in 1986, was a definite throwback to the old Convertible of the late Seventies. Between launch in October 1986 (the white car) and first production in summer 1987 (the dark-coloured car), the layout of the front doors and bonnet and their associated shut lines had been changed significantly, as had the road wheels. *(TVR)*

long gone. The problem now was not how to sell the cars that could be built, but how to build the cars that could be sold!

Although this was especially true of the S, the problem was that TVR were nowhere near ready to start building cars when the prototype was first shown in public. When I then visited TVR in October 1986, the first prototype car was still incomplete, and when it went on show at Birmingham's National Exhibition Centre this one and only car had not yet even turned a wheel. However, during the show, reaction was so positive that Peter Wheeler immediately ordered the car into production – and the work then *really* started!

If there was ever an excuse for stopping all work on the 420 Sports Saloon – which had also been previewed at the same show – this was it, though in truth no-one was interested in what was seen as an ungainly car. According to TVR at the time, if all had gone well the S should have gone into production in the spring of 1987, but this schedule was not

kept, as component shortages delayed 'Job One'.

Even though 60 orders had been received by March 1987, assembly was held up, first of all by a lack of petrol tanks, then by a shortage of door glass. Months came and went, and further detail styling revisions were made to the front end. In particular the bonnet/body shut lines were revised, which helped to make the bodyshell cheaper and easier to assemble. The result was a squat and purposeful sportscar, where the entire front half of the bodyshell, hinged in the nose, allowed the bonnet, complete with front wings, to lift up for access to the engine bay. Aft of the nose, the only break in the smooth lines was the inclusion of an asymmetric cool-air scoop in the bonnet top.

Only three cars were produced in the first half of the year, but in May 1987 series production was forecast to begin in July, and it was only then that the first 16 true production cars began to creep down the rudimentary assembly line in

Blackpool. At the time deliveries began in September the UK retail price had been held to the original forecast – £12,995 – and more than 150 customers – a quarter of TVR's annual production at the time – were already waiting. As the records show, just 89 cars – including one with a turbocharged engine – were built in 1987, but the rate of assembly was set to rocket in the coming months.

TVR was proud of the new S, not because it *was* new, but because it had been possible to bring it in at such a low price. At a stroke, it altered the balance of TVR's range. One reason, quite simply, was that this was an easier car to build than the Tasmin family – assembly took 250 man-hours compared with 400 man-hours for the 350i – which reduced labour costs considerably. Door glass had to be wound up and down by hand, leather upholstery was an optional extra, rear brakes were drums instead of discs, and there were other subtle cost-savings reflected in the price.

Even so, the engine and driveline were the same as that of the early-Eighties Tasmin, and expensive lace-web cast-alloy wheels were standard, as was the radio/cassette installation. It was a good-looking combination which many found attractive, and the order bank soon overwhelmed TVR's capacity to build cars.

Once the pundits and knowledgeable engineers could study the detail of the new S, they realized that not only its body style, but also its chassis-frame was totally different in detail from that of the Tasmin/350i family. Technically, the principal difference in the suspension was that there was a clever semi-trailing-arm layout at the rear, though the coil spring-over-shock absorber units were placed well forward and well away from the centre of the car to make sure they were located under the 'dead' area of the bodyshell, where they did not get in the way of the passenger compartment or the boot stowage area.

In looks, the new S seemed to be exactly what the market needed, for it was an altogether softer-looking TVR than the 280i (ex-Tasmin) that it replaced. Although it was thousands of pounds cheaper than the 280i, TVR didn't seem to have cut any corners, or eliminated anything. The door windows wound up and down smoothly, the soft-top – which was not

The S2 of 1988 looked much like the original, except for the simple and elegant eight-spoke alloy wheels. Under the bonnet, however, the latest type of Ford 2.9-litre V6 engine had been standardized. *(TVR)*

nearly as 'soft' as may be thought – included that excellent TVR feature of removable rigid roof sections and a fold-down roll hoop to give added security; most important of all, this ingenious assembly all seemed to be rainproof in the heaviest of inclement weather.

The facia was totally different from that of the 280i/350i family, but this was, shall we say, typical of TVR! This was the period in which dashboard layouts seemed to be changed regularly at Blackpool, so some observers suggested that it might not be around for long. They were right; by the time the V8S appeared, four years later, the facia looked entirely different.

The original S featured a deep central transmission tunnel – which was inevitable, because of the layout of the chassis-frame – with the padded vinyl facia moulding sweeping gracefully down over the passenger's legs to merge into the tunnel. Auxiliary instruments were aligned on that curve – it wasn't easy for the driver to read some of them as the steering wheel rim got in the way – and there was a confusing number of warning light lenses on the edge of the sweep, almost acting as 'stitches' for the upholstery. I never liked the layout, and I wasn't alone.

None of this seemed to matter, for a quick glance at the price lists proved how dramatically the arrival of the S had changed TVR's pricing structure. Once the car was launched, at £12,995 it was by far the cheapest UK-market TVR of the period; next up was the sharper-styled 350i, priced at £17,865, while the 390SE Convertible sold for £21,995.

Journalist Howard Lees of *Autocar* accurately picked up the flavour of TVR as a personally-owned company when he tried the car before an official road test car became available: "Climb into the S and one advantage of having Peter Wheeler in charge at TVR is obvious – at around six foot four he makes sure that the cars will fit taller drivers. The seats move back more than enough for my meagre six foot two and the 13in leather steering wheel is still well within reach.

"Just sit in the car and back you go 15 years. The seat is low and the curved windscreen wraps around and the traditional Smiths instruments reinforce the nostalgia. You look forward over a long, curved, bonnet with real, round, headlamps and a tasteful power bulge in the centre."

This was the S derivative which had every motoring writer foaming at the mouth – the 3.9-litre TVR Power/Rover V8-engined version, launched in 1991. Visually it was easy to 'pick' a V8S by the massive power bulge in the bonnet moulding, and yet another type of different road wheel. *(TVR)*

A few weeks later, the same magazine summed up its road test car as "Cheap, stylish and wonderful", and suggested that: "If only TVR can produce them fast enough, the S should ensure the company's survival. The car is quick, fun to drive and, on a quick straw poll around the office, looks sensational…".

Soon after these opinions were printed (in August and October 1987) the first deliveries of the new car were made, and by early 1988, with up to 10 cars a week being built, the S was already dominating the scene at Blackpool. More staff were taken on to deal with the rush, the cramped facilities were reshuffled as much as possible, and Wheeler set about planning his next new models. There was a certain urgency about this because the S killed off the 280i model at a stroke. In 1986 a total of 149 280i Convertibles had been built, but that figure plummeted to 31 in 1987. More significantly, the 280i was dropped as soon as S-series assembly began, there being effectively no overlap of the two cars.

In the meantime, there had already been one false start in

the S's evolution programme, for a car called the ES had been previewed at the 1987 Motorfair exhibition. The ES (or HPS, as it was briefly known) was further thinking on the theme of the new S, but this was a project which – like others at Blackpool at the time – went nowhere, and is more completely described in Chapter 8.

By mid-1988, only a year after the S had gone on sale, more than 50 cars were being produced every month, so it was no wonder that this was the year in which TVR production exceeded 700 cars for the very first time. It was the year in which 515 of the 701 cars built were S models – in other words, at this time, three out of every four newly-built TVRs were S models. All this, incidentally, was achieved *without*

trying to sell the cars into the American market, which Peter Wheeler had finally and irrevocably abandoned when he faced up to the burgeoning problems of product liability over there: "I would never sell cars to America again, because I regard it for this size of company as too unstable. The biggest problem of all is the public liability... I can remember that in 1986, I think it was, our product liability premium was $130,000. I got the renewal and I thought it was the same, but there was another nought on the end. How the hell can you plan?

"The only way I will sell cars to America again is if somebody comes and says, here is $5 million, and build a plant down the road. We'll make cars as long as it's got

By the time the S reached its third generation, the V8s had been launched, and the facia/instrument panel of these cars was much more elegant than before. But then, there was nothing which TVR enjoyed so much as playing around with different panel styles... *(TVR)*

When the S went on sale in 1987, the customers had a choice of facia. The vinyl padded facia was standard, but a wood veneer panel (same instrument layout) was an optional extra. *(TVR)*

The S3, S3C and S4C models, not forgetting the V8S, all had a smart facia which could not really have been more different from the original type. *(TVR)*

nothing to do with this company... They would sell like hot cakes in America now, but I am not going to involve this company in doing it. Now my export market is the South East of England, and it's much more reliable than any of the other export markets."

S2 and S2C – updating the Ford engineering

The original-specification S had a shorter career (13 months) than TVR would have liked mainly because Ford's policies obliged it to change the specification of the V6 engines used before the end of 1988. At least the necessary re-engineering was not too severe.

TVR, in fact, launched the S with what was still a current Ford engine in 1986, but that engine family was already under sentence of death at Ford (this, in fairness, was already known at TVR). By the time the car struggled into production the 160bhp 2.8-litre V6 engine was already obsolete at Ford, where it had been replaced by an evolutionary design. At the end of 1986 Ford had re-engineered its Granada/Scorpio models by discarding the old 2.3-litre and 2.8-litre

V6s in favour of a new generation of 2.4-litre and 2.9-litre types. As far as TVR and its customers were concerned, from 2,792cc to 2,933cc might sound like a trifling change, but it was actually rather more significant, as the new engines had entirely different cylinder heads and more advanced fuel injection systems.

Although the 2.9-litre kept the old 2.8-litre engine's cylinder bore, matched by a longer stroke – which guaranteed rather more low-speed and peak torque – 172lb.ft. instead of 162lb.ft. – it used entirely fresh cylinder head castings in which there were separate exhaust ports for each cylinder; the old heads, whose design dated from the Sixties when this was a 2-litre engine in the Taunus 20M, had always featured one pair of cylinders using siamesed ports, which restricted the breathing.

To help the engines meet all known exhaust emission regulations – this was important to Ford, for versions of the Cologne-built V6 engines were also fitted to various Ford-USA cars and light trucks – the old type of mechanical Bosch K-Jetronic fuel injection system had been discarded in favour

When working in GRP, it was always easy for TVR to get this sort of heavily contoured but delicate detail into the nose of their cars. *(TVR)*

of the more sophisticated electronically-controlled Bosch L-Jetronic system – used on some 2.8-litre types, but never those sold in the UK – which was linked to Ford's own EEC-IV electronic engine management system. In TVR guise, peak power was 168bhp, and the under-bonnet view looked different, though the twin inlets to the plenum were already familiar to Granada and Sierra XR4x4 owners.

TVR was delighted to have the use of this new engine, not only because it *was* new, but because it could run quite happily on leaded or unleaded fuel. The result was that it was now possible for the company to offer the S with a catalytic converter, this version being known as the S2C, which made

it more attractive in certain export markets. The bad news for TVR enthusiasts was that the S2 was considerably more costly than the original S – £15,450 instead of £12,995 – though TVR should at least have been praised for holding *down* the original S price during the rather elongated development period in 1987.

The S2 went on sale in the autumn of 1988, looking externally the same as before, and that controversially laid-out instrument panel was retained. There was now the option of a polished wood facia panel (surprisingly popular – TVR customers seemed to like their innovation linked to tradition) while instrument styling had been revised.

At the same time the rear suspension had been given a degree of 'anti-squat', which was intended to cut the chassis' tendency to rear up at the front under hard acceleration – but this habit was not eliminated entirely.

At first glance that price rise was a serious change – £2,455, or 19 per cent more than the original S1 – but it did not stop the car's success. Production at Blackpool continued at 40 per month or more, only being reduced in 1989 to allow more of the revitalized 400SE/450SE types to be made in its place.

S3 and S4C – continued success, with style and equipment improvements

TVR, as ever, did not sit back for long. No sooner had the S2 and S2C models gone into series production at the end of 1988 than the development team turned its attention to the body and its equipment, a series of improvements being made in the next few years which kept the Ford-engined car up to date as the seasons passed. From mid-1991, however, the publicity surrounding the birth of the new V8S overshadowed the original base-model V6-engined S, which outsold it considerably; the two cars shared the style and structural improvements which were made thereafter. By mid-1993, when yet more new TVR models – Griffith and Chimaera in particular – had come on the scene, V6 and V8 S types were selling equally well, the V8S having suffered most from the arrival of the Chimaera.

The S3 derivative of the early Nineties weighed in at £17,699 – without a catalyst – or £19,400 – as the S3C, complete with three-way catalyst. It looked similar externally to the S2 type, but in fact had 4in longer doors, and long-range driving lamps had been recessed below the bumper; this last frontal feature would also figure on the V8S when it appeared in 1991.

Inside the car there was a new style of facia – so that original type *had* been thought too radical, after all – with auxiliary instruments placed in a horizontal line in the centre of the car, the S3C also having an even higher interior specification, which included leather and walnut trim and electrically-operated door mirrors.

Gloom merchants pointed out that the S3 now cost 36 per cent more than the S1 had done when it was discontinued only two years earlier, a criticism which TVR ignored. The S3, after all, was still much the cheapest TVR in the 1990–91 range; the current 450SE, for instance, sold for £29,499, though admittedly very few of those cars were being sold.

TVR's customers clearly thought that the latest S model was exactly what they wanted, for by the end of 1990 the company was having to build more than 50 S-Series two-seaters every month to keep up with demand. In 1990 alone, TVR built 618 S-types, which was easily a single-model/single-year record for the company.

Seven years after it was launched, the V6-engined S, by this time labelled S4C, complete with catalytic converter, was still selling steadily – which, in motor industry-speak, means slowly – but until it was squeezed out of the available space at Bristol Avenue TVR seemed happy for it to continue.

By this time the windows were electrically operated (manual window drops could still be specified), the facia panel included a lot of walnut trim, rear-wheel braking was by discs, and a simple eight-spoke type of aluminium alloy road wheel was standard. After all that time, incidentally, there was no permanent hardtop option, as TVR had quite convinced its clientele about the merits of the fold-back roll-over bar and the use of twin Targa-type roof panels above their heads.

By 1991, though, the V6-engined cars had been out-gunned by the Rover V8-engined version of the same car, which TVR had put on sale in mid-year. The V8S, as it was known, was an even greater success than the original S had ever been.

The S, and the V8S models, had a neatly detailed rear-end style. *(TVR)*

V8S – the mighty Rover-engined version

Some people, it seems, are never satisfied. By the early Nineties, TVR dealers were having to deal with a stream of customers who said: "Look, I'd love to buy an S, but I want it to go as fast as my 350i. If only there was a V8-engined version of the car."

That message, repeated with ever more urgency from dealers who could see they were losing possible sales, soon got back to Blackpool. Before the Nineties, TVR was always constrained by the number of V8 engines which they could build for their own purposes, but in 1990 Peter Wheeler had bought up a Coventry-based engine-building company, NCK

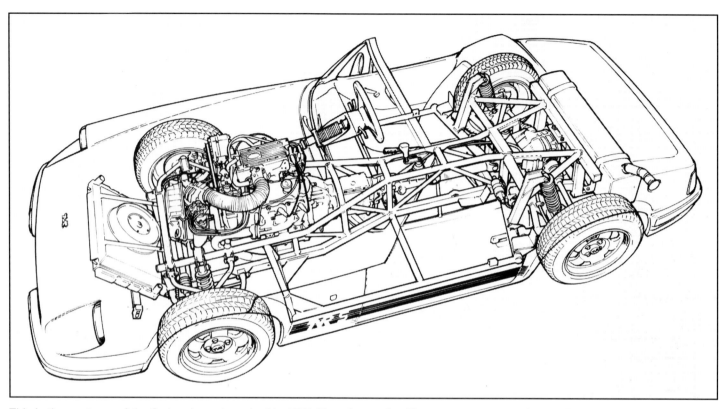

This is the anatomy of the S chassis, as launched in 1987. Note the semi-trailing-arm rear suspension, and the K-Jetronic fuel injection installation atop the 2.8-litre Ford V6 engine. *(TVR)*

Racing, which had been developed by TVR racing fanatic Allan Nash. Wheeler renamed it TVR Power, after which it was converted and expanded into the factory to modify and make more powerful all the Rover V8 engines which TVR needed. This would allow more engines to be made, one consequence being that a V8-engined S model was now feasible.

Without fanfares, but with deliveries beginning almost at once, TVR announced the V8S in mid-1991. Into the same basic body/chassis unit as the Ford V6-engined car, TVR inserted its own much-modified 3.95-litre version of the fuel-injected Rover V8 engine. The only visual change needed was to get rid of the scoop from the bonnet and produce a bulged moulding to provide proper clearance over the bulkier V8 engine's plenum chamber.

Rated at 240bhp, and backed by the familiar Rover five-speed gearbox and a 3.36:1 final-drive ratio, this rumbly but perfectly docile power unit turned the S from a fast sportscar into a *ferociously* fast sportscar, so it was a relief to see that it also had four-wheel disc brakes, 6.5in wheel rims and 205-

Even in four years the standard of trim and finish of the V8S had come a long way from that of the original S of 1987. *(TVR)*

section tyres.

In many ways the V8S was an uncouth extrovert of a machine – a throwback to the Griffith of the Sixties, though that name had already been allocated to the new-shape TVR 'Supercar' which would shortly go on sale, so predictably enough it became wildly popular! It had a 146mph top speed, the 0–100mph rubber-laying sprint took only 13.5 seconds, and the car had the sort of character which caused grown

men to reach for the open-necked shirts, Ray-Bans and medallions...

There were, however, limits beyond which TVR's marketing men were not prepared to go. Larger-capacity and considerably more powerful versions of the TVR Power/ Rover engine were already developed, but these were never made available in the V8S. Customers wanting much more power were politely but firmly steered in the direction of the Griffith or the Chimaera.

On announcement, the price of such self-indulgence started at £23,595. This was £3,480 less than the old 400SE Convertible, for which demand died away immediately. A look at the production records shows that the first V8S was built in August 1991 and that only three 400SEs were built after that. The V8S, though, was available with a long list of extras, which could lift the price much higher still; in 1993, when complete with a catalyst, TVR's price list for the V8S showed 20 optional extras. You could, for instance, have air conditioning (in an open car?), pedal boxes with increased *or* decreased legroom, central locking, gas-flowed cylinder heads...need I go on?

With such a combination of power, performance, style and sheer character, no wonder the V8S was popular. One of the UK's most forthright motoring magazines, *Fast Lane*, had the nerve to ask if the new car was the 'Poor man's Griffith?' – this being several months before the Griffith went on sale, and when the particular V8S road test car would have retailed at a cool £26,620!

The car itself – registered H15 VBS, which, if you read it quickly, could be HIS V8S – galvanized everyone who drove it. *Fast Lane* decided that: "Blackpool is responsible for more entertaining things than the Pleasure beach..." and: "If you can't quite afford a TVR Griffith, don't come running to us for sympathy. We'll give you several pieces of advice, one of which is to buy an S V8. Despite a few rough edges, it's a great car...".

Yet, by comparison with the sensational Griffith which followed (and gets a chapter to itself), the style of the V8S was beginning to look distinctly lumpy, but that didn't deter *Fast Lane* – which had not always seen eye-to-eye with TVR's management over previous models – from dripping with

enthusiasm over its character: "If you like to arrive unannounced you should buy something more restrained. Though the quality of the sound is music to anyone even mildly enthusiastic about cars, and though it isn't the sort of noise which rattles eardrums, there is no denying that the 400 engine is very loud indeed... In its overall behaviour, the [car] is much more civilized and capable than we expected... It's difficult to imagine that any real enthusiast would not succumb in a very short period to the charm of the V8S."

Autocar & Motor, testing the same car, was rather more equivocal, thinking it had incredible performance, but that it had a dreadful gearchange and was too noisy, with cramped footwells: "Even at idle, it makes enough noise to strike you off your neighbour's Christmas card list, and much more than 3,000rpm in a built-up area is plain anti-social." On the other hand, the summary was that: "On an empty, dry road, the TVR V8S puts a smile on your face that, for the money, little else can approach. It is as quick to 60mph as a [Ferrari] Testarossa and a sight more wieldy down a country lane...

TVR has provided a fine ride, spacious cabin and large boot. But until it is made quieter, the V8S will be neither a comfortable long-distance cruiser nor a sensible everyday car."

Was it any wonder that, after this reception, the demand for the V8S took off considerably; 47 cars were made in September 1991, and again in October 1991, and until the Griffith finally went on sale at the start of 1992 the V8S was TVR's best-selling model. It wasn't until the Griffith's fabulous reputation became known that the V8S's popularity receded. However, fame is ephemeral. A year after V8S deliveries began, production was down to only 10 cars per month, this dropping even further in the winter of 1992–93.

By that time, indeed, the basic style of the S4C and V8S models had been around for six years – or if you recall the Seventies' models on which the shape was based, it had been around for about 15 years. By current TVR standards, that is an awfully long time to leave a car alone, so it was certain that more change, perhaps a completely new model, would soon take over.

CHAPTER 5

420SEAC and Tuscan

With motor racing in mind – 1986 and 1988

Peter Wheeler and Stewart Halstead were both motor racing enthusiasts, so whenever the chance came to develop an ultra-special TVR model they jumped at it. In the late Eighties two such models appeared, made a number of headlines for the company and then faded away into the background. Both of these cars relied on the remarkable light-alloy Rover V8 engine to give them competitive straight-line performance. Improvements to the TVR chassis, and changes to the body style, saw to the rest.

In the early Eighties TVR became ever more closely involved in British production sportscar racing and, starting with the 350i Convertible, a whole series of technical improvements were made to the chassis.

Development of the powerplant began in 1984, and it wasn't long before an enlarged (3,905cc) Rover engine was developed. Naturally, TVR also made this available in a production car, the result of this line of development being the birth of the 390SE.

Chassis changes included adopting ventilated front disc brakes, four-pot brake calipers and a series of revisions to the suspension. The rear suspension, in particular, needed to be made more precise, the result being the fitment of a new four-point-mounted lower wishbone, along with a torque reaction arm to the chassis.

Two factory-sponsored 390SEs raced at many British circuits in 1985, the season being marked by the use of a yet-larger engine (the long-stroke 4,228cc unit), and by the testing of a free-standing rear spoiler to help trim the aerodynamics. Changes to the vehicle's overall shape were then considered,

this being the point at which the 390SE race car really evolved into a new machine, the 420SEAC.

420SEAC

This model evolved in direct response to a demand from TVR customers for a new 'flagship' style, with more power, better roadholding and better aerodynamics. Almost by definition, the result was likely to be a limited-production machine, and if the price was to be high, so be it. Peter Wheeler was convinced that if the car was good enough, there would be no shortage of customers. In any case, the car's specification was so advanced, and the performance potential so startling, that the £29,500 price tag looked very reasonable indeed.

The car's title hid one of the principal changes, for 'SEAC' stood for Special Equipment Aramid Composite, which referred to the material used to build the bodyshells. Based on the well-known 390SE shell, which used a glassfibre composite material, the 420SEAC style was not only redeveloped to feature a shorter and more rounded nose, flared arches, pronounced side skirts and a separate rear spoiler panel, but much of the new panelling was constructed in Aramid materials with a significant proportion of Kevlar – which is stronger, lighter, but admittedly more costly than ordinary glassfibre.

The race cars were the first to use the new style of independent rear suspension which has already been mentioned, and that fitted to the 420SEAC was the same as on other 1986-model TVRs. In addition, wheel rim widths

The 420SEAC model, officially put on sale in October 1986, had its body style developed in a factory-backed racing programme. Not only was the nose shorter and more rounded than that of the 390SE, but there were 'runningboards' along the side, and an aerofoil section behind the cockpit. *(TVR)*

increased to 8.5in, allied to 225-section Bridgestone tyres, ventilated front disc brakes with four-pot calipers, power-assisted steering as standard, and detail changes to the front geometry, springs and damper rates were all added to the specification.

Although based on the rugged and successful Rover 3½-litre V8 design, the 420SEAC unit was even further developed and modified than the 309SE's engine had been. For this application it had a 93.5mm bore and a 77mm stroke, which produced a capacity of 4,228cc, and in standard form no less than 300bhp was developed at 5,500rpm, with a staggering 290lb.ft of torque at 4,500rpm. In this form TVR claimed that the 420SEAC was capable of 165mph, with 0–60mph acceleration in 5sec. Nor was that all, for race-tuned engines with an extra 85bhp, produced by dry-sump lubrication, modified manifolding and reground camshaft profiles, could also be supplied.

The first 420SEAC prototype began racing at the beginning of 1986, and was soon so successful that it was banned from motorsport by the governing authorities! Quite simply,

it was too fast for its opposition – but that was the sort of reputation which TVR thought they could live with.

The production car was launched in October 1986, where its claimed top speed of up to 165mph caused many a gasp. However, although it was clearly a formidable machine, particularly when supplied with the most powerful version of the 4.2-litre engine, it was also very expensive. The initial price of £29,500 was considerably higher than that of any other current TVR – the 390SE, for instance, cost £21,995.

The price level, and the rather idiosyncratic styling, ensured that demand would always be low. According to TVR's own chassis records, only four cars were produced in 1986, another 14 followed in 1987, and a steady trickle of 19 were then built in 1988. Most of these cars were bought with motorsport in mind, and on the track the 420SEAC could be a formidable machine.

Classic & Sportscar's editor, Mark Hughes, got his hands on a white 420SEAC early in 1987, described it succinctly as "White Lightning", raved about the straight-line performance, and wrote: "The TVR seems...razor-sharp, with a turn-in ability which has it darting in to corners more quickly than you anticipate. The bonus of that firm ride is that the 420SEAC is rock-steady in corners, with virtually no roll and appreciably more poise than the 350i. Where the 350i had given a little twitch at the rear when you jumped on the power, the 420SEAC kept a true line, just tightening a fraction... Above all, the lasting impression is that it has almost no equal as a genuinely high-performance convertible. Few cars can match its capabilities, but even fewer allow you to experience this level of performance while enjoying the sun on your head...".

When the company's own works race car, a canary yellow-coloured monster with no less than 365bhp from its specially-tuned engine, was tested by motor-noters from *Motor* and *Autocar* (they were still separate journals then) in 1987, the superlatives flowed even faster. This particular machine was Steve Cole's car, who had already won scores of races in other formulae, notably when driving a Rover-powered Morgan Plus 8, and had won 19 races from 24 starts in 1986 when the car's specification was so controversial.

TVR's competitions programme was directed by Chris Schirle, one-time general manager of Broadspeed. As Schirle

The nose of the 420SEAC had an altogether softer profile than that of the 390SE and, from this angle at least, looked very pleasing indeed. (TVR)

Announced in 1980, the Tasmin Convertible soon became the best seller in the TVR range. This is an early-specification 1981 model.

TVR's range was widening fast by the mid-Eighties. These four models, clockwise from nearest to the camera, are the 390SE, the 280i, the 350i Coupe and the 350i Convertible.

Rear view of the 420SEAC model, showing the free-standing aerofoil section mounted on the bootlid and the new shape of rear bumper/spoiler. *(TVR)*

pointed out to *Motor*'s intrepid tester at the Oulton Park circuit: "It is not a toy. It is a serious motor car. You have to treat it with respect." In addition: "Don't use more than 6,200rpm – just use the torque. You won't need fifth."

Clearly the race-prepared 420SEAC was a remarkable machine, but the tester soon noticed something else: "One of the curious aspects of driving a V8 is that...they often don't *feel* very fast. It is only when you get to the end of a straight, with the next corner looming, that you realize how rapidly you have been propelled from the last corner...".

Several near-accidents later – in a car which was due to race for TVR only a few days later – the intrepid correspondent summarized, briskly: "Peter Wheeler's company makes *fast* cars."

Autocar's Graham Jones and Andrew Kirk were no less impressed by the same car, which they tried at Silverstone. Calling the standard machine the "King Kong of the TVR range", they contented themselves by taking straight-line

acceleration figures: "On slicks, acceleration is especially vivid, though trying to transmit 365bhp through to the rear wheels, even in the dry, results in considerable wheelspin when accelerating hard from rest. Even so, 30mph appears in only 1.9secs and 60mph in a very rapid 4.6secs. The engine is only just getting into its stride at this point and goes on to 100mph in a mere 10.7secs. Top speed depends entirely on the chosen gearing but the test vehicle managed a mean of 147mph at 6,500rpm on the day...".

This was impressive stuff, and the short-lived 450SEAC which was built in 1988 and 1989 was even more ferocious. With a simple engine change – the latest long-stroke 4,441cc version of the Rover engine, with a colossal 324bhp even in so-called standard form, was fitted – this was a car for which TVR charged £33,950 in 1988, and of which only 18 examples were produced. The last 450SEAC was produced in June 1989, by which time the TVR spotlight had moved decisively to the brand-new Tuscan model.

Although the 420SEAC had a unique, rounded, nose, sills and rear bumper, it was still recognizably based on the current Convertible style. Strangely, there is no rear spoiler on this example – it could be deleted on request. *(TVR)*

Tuscan

Two years after the 420SEAC had burst on the British sportscar scene, TVR performed another conjuring trick. The best way to summarize the launch of a new machine called the Tuscan is to quote from the company's own press release of August 1988: "Tuscan – a name from the past. A challenge for the future. New models and £30,000 in prize money... The new model will be called Tuscan – named after

one of the fastest TVRs ever built back in the 1960s. To coincide with the launch of the Tuscan, TVR will also be unveiling a specially-equipped race version to compete in a one-make challenge to run throughout 1989 – called The Tuscan Challenge.

"The Tuscan will be based on the TVR S Convertible... however, in true TVR fashion, the Tuscan provides extended performance and specification...".

The 390SE Series 2 was a development of a style first seen in 1980, but the 'retro-look' S seen in the backround, which went on sale in 1987, was much cheaper and proved a runaway success.

Not all 420SEACs were race cars! This was the very smart wood-trimmed interior of a left-hand-drive example. TVR dashboards have been changed constantly over the years.

TVR previewed the new Tuscan model at the NEC motor show of 1988 with this brave display. The prototype road car was supposed to anticipate production beginning in 1989, but in the end Tuscans were only used for racing. *(TVR)*

In the beginning, TVR had thought to promote the Challenge for only mildly-tuned (250bhp) versions of the engine, but this idea was soon ditched in favour of an 'anything goes' formula. The cars were offered for sale at an amazingly low price – £16,000 plus VAT – but one requirement was that each car had to compete in at least six of the Challenge's 12 races. If not, TVR was ready to send out a further invoice – for £16,000!

Based on the S Convertible? When it was to be a fire-breathing successor to the 420SEAC? Nowadays, I'm sure, Peter Wheeler would agree that this was stretching a point. The engine owed more to the 350i than to the S, there was an unfamiliar gearbox, the chassis was different, the wheelbase and tracks were both increased, and the styling was much changed. Based on the S Convertible? It depended on whether you were a company publicist or an engineer!

Because this was to be a brand-new model, intended to be the flagship of the range, TVR designed a completely new chassis-frame. Drawing on the experience gained with the two other Eighties-types – the Tuscan/350i type, and the S type – the frame was more rigid than ever before, with accurately located wheels at front and rear. Right from the start it was designed to cope with as much power and torque as any tuning shop could extract from the Rover V8 engine.

In general layout the Tuscan's frame looked familiar. The basis was a four-tube backbone section, flared and cross-braced at the front to embrace the Rover engine, and rigidly profiled at the rear to surround the differential. Front and rear suspensions were both by wide-based unequal-length wishbones, with coil-over-shock absorber installations. There seemed to be thoughtfully positioned little metal fillets everywhere to add rigidity and stop any tendency of the sections to 'lozenge'.

Because a completely new chassis jig was needed, there was no point in sticking with existing wheelbase/track dimensions. For the new Tuscan, therefore, the wheelbase was 7ft 8in –

mid-way between the 7ft 6in of the S and the 7ft 10in of the 350i – while the tracks were 4ft 10.3in, the widest seen on a TVR. The wheels on the race car had 9in rims; road-car wheels would inevitably have been narrower, but such a derivative was never produced.

In the beginning, as emphasized by the dramatic motor show stand display at the NEC, two versions of the car were proposed, one for road use, the other for use in the Tuscan Challenge. The road car, though still ferociously powerful, could not hold a candle to the race car, which used yet another variation of the Rover V8 theme, this being the long-stroke 4.4-litre unit; as raced in 1989, a typical power output

One sure way to advertise TVR's engine-tuning skills was to placard one of the Tuscan Challenge race cars. *(TVR)*

TVR Tuscans (reviving an earlier model name) went on sale as race cars in 1989. Their style was unique, purposeful and very impressive.

When launched in 1986 the 420SEAC was the most powerful TVR so far put on sale, but only 37 of them were built over two years before the even more powerful 450SEAC took over.

The Tuscan Challenge has excited – sometimes frightened – crowds and drivers from 1989 into the Nineties. When the Tuscans race, the ground trembles... *(TVR)*

was 400bhp at 7,500rpm, the peak torque being a stump pulling 360lb.ft at 5,500rpm.

Because the company knew that the engines would be tuned to produce up to 400bhp in racing trim, the five-speed Rover gearbox was not specified, the American Borg-Warner T5 five-speed gearbox, as fitted in rear-drive Sierra RS Cosworth and Sierra RS500 Cosworth road cars, being chosen instead. To historians and number crunchers it was a very familiar 'building block', of which literally millions had already been built; introduced in 1980, it had been used in various American Motors, General Motors, Nissan, Isuzu and Ford-USA models.

In hindsight, the styling, mainly influenced by Peter Wheeler himself, was a logical development of that found in the S *and* it was an ancestor of that later to be seen on the Griffith. It was altogether more rounded than any previous TVR had been, with faired-in headlamps and a chopped-off tail.

This revealing cutaway features the 1992 4.3-litre version of the Griffith, which was TVR's best-selling car that year. Produced by technical illustrator Myles Talbot, the drawing can also be obtained as a limited-edition print direct from the artist at 1 Warren Drive, Eldwick, Bingley, West Yorkshire BD16 3BX.

The Chimaera, new on the market in 1993, used much of the Griffith's chassis and running gear, but it had different styling and was somewhat cheaper to buy.

Compared with all other TVRs except the 420SEAC/450SEAC, the Tuscan was equipped with larger, wider tyres and wider-rim wheels – but for motor racing purposes this did not impress the drivers much at all! Frankly (and purposely – for Wheeler wanted to make this an exciting form of motor racing) the racing Tuscan was under-tyred and under-braked, and the very strict rules of the Challenge meant that there was no solution to the problem.

The alloy 9in rims might look meaty enough for road work, but when up to 400bhp – with more to come in future years – had to be transmitted to the track through the rear wheels, they were almost laughably narrow – the result being cars which were blood-curdlingly fast in a straight line, but whose handling was a throw-back to the Seventies (even, some said, to the Sixties).

The financial deal offered by TVR was so attractive that there was no problem in selling all the cars and ensuring full grids for a British one-make series. No fewer than 35 cars were assembled in the spring of 1989, and several other examples were to follow in the succeeding winters.

The first 1989 race, at Donington Park, attracted 21 starters, and spectators soon realized that to be a winning driver it also helped to be a touch crazy. *Fast Lane* editor Peter Dron, who drove in that first race, later wrote: "We are just as mad as the men from TVR, and really ought to be kept in rooms with rubber wallpaper…".

Later, confirming the limitations of the car, he commented: "I stayed hard on the power, and then braked ludicrously late and very hard. At this point the Tuscan must have been pulling 140 or 150mph. The front brakes faded out instantly, the rears locked, and I went from lock to lock desperately to keep the car pointed in a straight line…

"These Tuscans are *seriously* fast, as might be expected from nearly 400bhp in a car weighing around 800kg [Really? That was much lighter than claimed at launch – AAGR]. Just how fast is indicated by the fact that Jeff Allam…is only a couple of seconds off Andy Rouse's Group A record in his 500bhp Sierra Cosworth… With softer slicks, obviously the TVRs would instantly be a few seconds quicker, but I think the choice of relatively hard Dunlops was a wise one… The cars have improved enormously since testing began, but they are still fairly difficult to drive…".

Chris Schirle, one-time TVR development engineer, who moved out to prepare the Tuscan owned by David Gerald TVR and driven in that first season by veteran Gerry Marshall, had very firm opinions about the cars: "They're absolute monsters. All the cars are unstable under braking and it's so easy to swop ends."

It was no wonder that Tuscans regularly went off the road, spun out, or crashed into each other – sometimes all at the same time – but there was no doubt about one thing – the Challenge won a lot of attention. One race at Silverstone, early in the season, saw a crash which involved no fewer than eight cars. That was a record, but it was a rare race when less than five or six cars dropped out! More than 25 cars started most races, but there was a lot of carnage. Although the cars were good value to buy, upkeep tended to be expensive.

At the end of the first year experienced drivers like Jeff Allam – who won the Challenge in the R A Potter car – Chris Hodgetts, Steve Cole and Gerry Marshall took the honours, but (as *Autosport* wrote in its seasonal review): "…there was an unnerving disparity between the front and the tail of the grid…the cars made a fine spectacle, but it left you wondering about the wisdom of allowing novices into the challenge."

At the end of the 1990 season, *Autosport* commented: "There is no doubt that the TVR Tuscan Challenge is a place for the gifted or the brave. In its second season, the 400bhp one-make series to beat all one-make series again comprehensively sorted the men from the boys. That Chris Hodgetts went one better on his 1989 runner-up slot came as little surprise to anybody."

Chris drove The Sports Car Centre's machine, and won six of the first eight races, but in the end John Kent – driving for the TVR Centre – ran him very close. Gerry Marshall only rarely raced, and Steve Cole took third place.

Chris Hodgetts did not defend his title in 1991, but familiar names – including Steve Cole, who won the Challenge, Colin Blower, Gerry Marshall and John Kent – all appeared. This seemed to be *the* series for well-known names like the McRaes, Tiff Needell and Chris Hodgetts to come 'guesting', and everyone had fun, though the cars were no

Big car, big man, big performance – Gerry Marshall driving one of the Tuscan Challenge race cars in his usual extrovert way. All the cars had to comply with the same set of regulations. *(TVR)*

Racing TVRs came in all shapes, sizes and colours. In the late Eighties David Gerald Racing supported a 420SEAC and a late Seventies' 3000S. *(TVR)*

easier to drive than before.

By 1992 the cars were beginning to creak a little, but re-preparation, development, and the supply of new chassis and even a few new cars helped to keep the grids full, and the racing was as exciting as ever. Even by 1993, when the series might have been expected to be dying of neglect, there was still a great deal of interest, excitement and close competition. TVR stalwarts like Steve Cole and Colin Blower were ever-presents, and journalists like Mark Hales and John Barker became closely involved, while TVR's Chairman Peter Wheeler also put his reputation where his money already was and raced regularly against his customers.

What next for the Tuscan? More motor racing, a new model carrying the same name but a different style? Or a dignified withdrawal from motorsport? With TVR, anything can happen…

CHAPTER 6

Griffith

The shapely TVR for the Nineties

Of all current superlatives lavished upon the Griffith it was *Autocar & Motor* who best summed-up the car as: "So close to greatness, it hurts…".

Everyone – and I have searched high and low to find any heretics – loved the Griffith production car, not only for its looks, but for its performance and road behaviour. Only one production figure alone need be quoted – the 602 cars produced in 1992 alone – which proves that the buying public loved it as much as the pundits. Quite simply, in its first year so many Griffiths were sold that all other TVR models had to fight for space in corners of the crowded factory. In that year, Griffith build accounted for 73 per cent of TVR production.

Even so, TVR were either lucky, or calculatingly ingenious, to end up with such a stunningly capable machine, for the car which went on sale in 1992 was rather different from the prototype shown in 1990. In the 15 months between preview and sale, the Griffith was given a totally different chassis and there were subtle but nevertheless extensive styling modifications. The car which went on sale was more capable, and somehow had an even more aggressive character than the prototype.

The Griffith was born to answer demands for an S with a V8 engine, so at the same time a new body style was considered. This was also the period when Peter Wheeler was continuing his quest to develop a new model to replace the old Tasmin-based 350i/400SE/450SE range. His first attempt, with the Speed Eight of 1989, had already faltered, for the 1990 version of that car was destined to be a 2+2, not a two-seater like all the late-model Tasmin-family models. Still looking for a Supercar, and trying to keep all his dealers happy, he set out to try again, and decided to revive the famous Griffith name.

At the time – mid-1990 – TVR were not prepared to design a completely new car. Two types of TVR chassis were currently in series production, and for the time being the new car would have to be based on one of them. The 350i/400SE/450SE type was a development of the Tasmin, and was therefore a decade old. The S-Series was modern (the first S models had been delivered in 1987), but had been designed and built down to a price to make it a bargain two-seater. Neither chassis, therefore, looked ideal as the basis for a new 150mph TVR.

For the first car, TVR chose to use an S-Series chassis with the 3.9-litre Rover engine installed – in effect this was a prototype V8S chassis, although *that* car would not go on sale until the summer of 1991.

The new car's body style, which was influenced by Wheeler and John Ravenscroft, was radically new. Nothing so sensuous or so brutally aggressive had ever before been seen on a TVR, and when exhibited at the Birmingham (NEC) motor show it caused a sensation. At one time during that show, the staff were logging an order every eight minutes. Some eager customers were ready to pay substantial deposits there and then in order to secure early delivery. By the end of the show more than 350 people had said they wanted to buy the Griffith.

Wheeler, however, had become uneasy about the specifica-

tion. The only prototype, after all, was effectively a rebodied V8S, and there were still some elements of the style he thought could be improved. Most important, by upgrading the design he could also make it unique and, in industry-speak, he could 'position' it further away from the S model, in image and in price.

The original non-running prototype, therefore, was returned to Blackpool, where a wholesale reappraisal took place. Development of a V8-engined S (described in Chapter 4) was finalized, with sales beginning during 1991, while the Griffith was completely redesigned.

Interviewed by Mark Hughes for *Autocar & Motor* in 1991, Peter Wheeler described what caused this: "At the time we first showed the Griffith, I was becoming concerned by the number of people approaching TVR Power, our sister company, and asking for bigger and more highly tuned engines.

"The S chassis has the ability to handle the power of the new V8S model, but not dramatically higher outputs. I decided that the Griffith's design had to start again on the chassis side.

"Since this caused a delay, I finally decided to re-engineer the entire car. So we went right back to square one last January [1991]. The Griffith now represents the state of the art for us, and in certain areas is more complex than anything we've ever built."

Back to square one meant ditching the S chassis and electing to use a lightly-modified version of the racing Tuscan assembly instead. The Tuscan design was not only stiffer and more capable of handling very high power output and torque, but it had totally different front and rear suspension. There were wide-based and properly-located unequal-length wishbones at each end of the car. In this form the new car had more rigidly supported wheels, which could have wider rims, and at a very early stage it was also decided to fit 15in

Not a curve, crease or detail out of place: the sensational Griffith which went on sale in 1992. *(TVR)*

It was possible – just – to stow the Griffith's removable roof panel in the boot, but many owners chose to leave it at home, and chance the weather... *(TVR)*

diameter wheels at the front and 16in at the rear.

Even if TVR had been happy with the original Griffith style, they were still forced to alter it to accommodate the new chassis. A totally different floorpan moulding was required in any case, and although it was simple enough to shorten the Tuscan's frame by 2in (the Tuscan wheelbase was 92in, that of the Griffith 90in), other changes were needed to accommodate the wider tracks and the different-size rear wheel/tyre combination.

The Griffith production car, therefore, whilst looking superficially identical to that of the 1990 prototype, was subtly different in every line, profile and contour. By comparison with the V8S, or the old 400SE, it was exceedingly sleek and rounded.

Straight lines and sharp edges had been completely banished, as had almost any excrescence which was not imposed on TVR by legislation.

Wheeler bravely elected to do away completely with front or rear bumpers, which automatically helped the style, and the only two features which could be called 'styling' rather than 'engineering' were the recessed edges of the bonnet panel and the way the front edge of the doors was moulded inboard of the back of the front wings. The door handles were concealed in the moulding aft of the doors, rather than in the doors themselves, and the removable Targa roof panel was single-piece, rather than two-piece like the S model.

Inside the car, too, there were curves everywhere. The facia swept more than halfway across the car, the centre console

Like the rest of the car, the facia/instrument panel of the 1992 Griffith was a study in curves. *(TVR)*

seductively surrounded the gear-lever and the handbrake, and the trim panels of the doors also clung sinuously to the mouldings. The boot was wide and deep, if not conspicuously long, and there were neat little touches like the aluminium-alloy gear knob and the recessed front driving lamps.

The engine/driveline combination looked familiar to all TVR lovers, for there was a choice of TVR Power/Rover V8 engines, backed by the usual five-speed all-synchromesh gearbox. The engine was well back in the chassis, which should have made for a lot of underbonnet space, but although a catalyst-equipped exhaust system was envisaged – the catalysts taking up a great deal of space towards the front of the engine bay – this was not immediately available, there was no automatic transmission option – such non-sporting nonsenses had been swept away in 1986 – and the rack-and-pinion steering was unassisted.

With 3.95 litres and 240bhp the Griffith looked to be staggeringly fast, but with the optional 4.3 litres and 280bhp there was promise of truly amazing performance. All this, combined with looks that any other maker of Supercars would kill for, promised to make the Griffith irresistible.

In October 1991 no fewer than three pre-production Griffiths were on display at the Motorfair (London) motor show, prices of 4-litre and 4.3-litre versions had been announced, and deliveries were forecast to begin during the winter, when 12 cars would be built every week. It was the quoted prices which finally convinced sportscar lovers that they had to buy a Griffith. Naturally the 4-litre Griffith was more costly than the V8S, but it was quite a lot *cheaper* than the old 400SE, which was just breathing its last. Here are the relevant 1991 prices:

V8S	(4-litre engine)	£23,595
Griffith 4.0	(4-litre engine)	£25,795
400SE	(4-litre engine)	£28,495

TVR production in full swing at Bristol Avenue in 1992. A Griffith is in the foreground, with Griffith chassis being assembled on the right. There is a long way to go before the finished car is ready for delivery. *(TVR)*

The Griffith/Chimaera type of front suspension evolved from that of the Tuscan race cars, and had sturdy, wide-based wishbones and massive brake calipers. *(TVR)*

Reminding its readers that it accelerated faster than a Ferrari Testarossa or a Porsche 911 Turbo, the testers summarized: "With the Griffith, TVR might just have rewritten the rule book on sports cars for all time, just as Jaguar did with the E-Type more than 30 years ago. The car's list of tangible assets – thundering performance, fabulous looks, a £27,000 price tag and its build quality (a first for the small Blackpool-based company) – reads even more like a fairy tale than *Alice in Wonderland* ever did.

"The Griffith is so much better than any previous TVR in terms of its general cabin ergonomics that it's sometimes hard to believe it originates from the same source."

It was even faster than forecast, for the magazine recorded a top speed of 161mph, and among many outstanding acceleration figures was the ability to thunder up to 100mph in a mere 11.1sec ("Few experiences on earth can prepare you for what happens when a Griffith goes on full reheat..."). Tut-tutting columnists in some newspapers thought this was just about as immoral as could be – but the fans loved it.

If there was a flaw, however small, it was in the exhaust

Production got under way at the end of 1991, the first deliveries, all to home-market customers, being made early in 1992. Up to 12 cars a week were promised at first, but by mid-year this figure had edged up to 15 cars a week, and demand showed no signs of easing. The first thing that became clear was that *every* customer was opting for the larger and more powerful engine option. This suited TVR very well, for it served to place the Griffith even further away, in image terms, from the V8S model.

At the time the Griffith was put on sale in 1992, it was the most important single model in TVR's line-up, so understandably the staff were anxious that the motoring press would like the car. They did not have long to wait.

Autocar & Motor described the 4.3-litre car as: "Unbelievably quick, spectacular looking, but not for the faint-hearted."

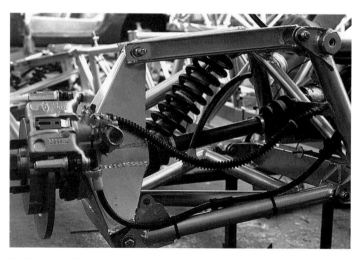

Griffith and Chimaera models shared the same type of wishbone rear suspension. Surprisingly, solid disc brakes were good enough to keep the colossal performance of these cars in check. *(TVR)*

The Griffith/Chimaera chassis frame (foreground) looks superficially like earlier TVR designs, but in this case the suspension layout and sturdy mountings are a reminder that it was originally developed for use under the Tuscan. The dark-painted frame in the background is for an S model. *(TVR)*

noise (too loud) and the handling, where the Griffith occasionally seemed to lose its rear-end composure. But with 280bhp on tap, and such startling acceleration on offer, most people forgave it for that and decided to drive like mere mortals instead of trying to imitate Ayrton Senna or Alain Prost.

Mark Hales and Andrew English of *Performance Car*, who tested the self-same car (J524 MHG), were almost as ecstatic. Dubbing the Griffith the "Blackpool Flyer", they reported similar performance figures, while at the same time cooing over the exhaust noise: "The noise is all one would expect of a TVR, and if your greenhouse implodes in sympathetic vibration, you can always specify the exhaust system...". The heavy steering was criticized – one might even say they banged on about this – but: "All in all it must be the best designed and finished TVR ever produced... What a charming car. It has all the power one would ever want for the road, all the looks, all the comfort."

There was much more in this vein, the result merely being to confirm the latent demand for the Griffith model.

Throughout the year production built up steadily to keep abreast with orders, almost all of them from UK dealers; 35 cars were built in February 1993, 60 in March, a record 65 in June, and between 50 and 60 every month for the rest of the year.

Then, perversely as it seemed at first, TVR announced that they were to turn off the tap, to withdraw the Griffith from the UK market for the time being. Were they crazy, the pundits wanted to know? Not according to Chairman Peter Wheeler.

There were several reasons: to allow the export market – which only accounted for about 15 per cent of TVR's sales at this time – its turn with the Griffith; to finalize the catalyst installation for UK-market cars; to pave the way for a slightly cheaper derivative of this chassis – the Chimaera. Also on the horizon was the introduction of the new AJP8 engine, which promised to be more powerful than any Rover-derived engine so far put into a TVR production car, and which Wheeler intended would go into the 1993 Griffith model.

Sure enough, although there was still an extremely healthy demand for the cars, production of UK-market non-catalytic-conversion cars was suspended in December 1992, the result being that at the beginning of 1993 Griffith production dropped like a stone. Only 10 cars were produced in February 1993 and a mere five in April – but by then the new Chimaera had arrived and the TVR factory was still bursting at the seams.

Then came a typically rapid TVR change of mind and realignment of policy. With AJP8 engine development dragging its feet early in 1993, well beyond the original start-up date (see next chapter), and British TVR dealers still screaming for Griffiths to sell, Wheeler decided to bring it back again, still with a Rover-derived engine; the revised car, badged Griffith 500, appeared in August 1993.

Having promised that the 1993 Griffith-AJP model would have 4.2 litres and more than 360bhp, his engineers needed to do something outstanding with the ageing pushrod V8.

This time – and surely this *had* to be the last major change made to the Rover engine by TVR Power – the capacity was increased from the 4.5 litres used in earlier models to the full 5-litre capacity for which this cylinder block had always been designed way back in the Sixties.

This was done by leaving the bore at 94mm, but lengthening the stroke to 90mm. Power *and* torque increases were impressive, for with no less than 325bhp on tap the latest Griffith 500 promised to be more fierce than almost any previous TVR model.

At the same time Wheeler and his associates found time to dabble with a facelift. Although the general style was left alone, the nose was altered so that the extra driving lamps were incorporated into the air intake recess, while the smooth but simple OZ wheel pattern already seen on other 1993 TVRs was also standardized.

The AJP8-powered derivative would need to be truly outstanding to outpace this model.

Head-on view of a Griffith/Chimaera rolling chassis being assembled at Blackpool. The painted number on the crossmember tells the work-force that it has already been allocated an identity. Within two weeks, it will be part of a complete car on its way to a customer. *(TVR)*

Non-runners. The original Griffith concept car of 1990, lined up in front of BAe's European Fighter Aircraft prototype. Both have come a long way since then! *(TVR)*

TVR enthusiasts will probably recognize this as a pre-production Griffith of 1991, which has still to lose its exterior door handles, have its side-repeater indicators added and the road-wheel design changed. The wonderfully attractive and sensuous styling lines, though, have already been established. *(TVR)*

The Griffith could be ordered in one of many body colours, but its swooping lines look particularly good in softer shades such as an attractive metallic green-blue. *(TVR)*

For 1994 the Griffith was re-engineered, becoming the 5-litre TVR-Power-engined Griffith 500. The only style changes were concentrated around the nose, which was more integrated than before. (TVR)

The 1994-model Griffith 500, complete with modern-pattern road wheels, looked as wickedly fast as would be expected. With 325bhp on tap, the performance was almost unimaginable! (TVR)

CHAPTER 7

Chimaera and a new AJP8 engine

New style, in-house power – and more to come

During 1992 TVR worked feverishly to prepare themselves for the NEC motor show, where in October they intended to launch yet another new model and to preview their brand-new own-design engine. The strategy, which was to be badly dented by time, was that the new engine, dubbed AJP8, should be used in a redeveloped Griffith in order to fill the marketing gap between the V8S and the existing Griffith.

Although the master plan was knocked askew during 1993 because AJP8 engine development took much longer than forecast, the new model, named Chimaera, was an instant success.

Chimaera – design and development

This was the first time since 1980 that TVR had produced a new model name – both the Tuscan race car and the Griffith had recycled the names invented at TVR in the financially rocky Sixties. As soon as we saw the new car, we dashed for our dictionaries to see what the name meant. Apparently one of Peter Wheeler's customers had suggested it, but Wheeler must surely have hesitated before he adopted it?

'Chimera' (also spelt Chimaera) is variously defined as: referring back to Greek mythology to describe a fire-breathing female monster with a lion's head, a goat's body and a serpent's tail; a fantastic or grotesque product of the imagination – a bogey; any fabulous beast with parts taken from various animals.

Whether or not this makes it any clearer, only TVR could have adopted it. It is difficult to imagine Ford, Rover or General Motors putting a new product on the market where the cynics could have referred to it as a 'grotesque product' or a 'bogey'!

TVR's idea was to capitalize on the success of the Griffith, but to make the new car slightly 'softer' and more practical, without slashing the selling price. Even though much of the chassis and running gear, hidden from view, was like that of the Griffith, the body style was noticeably different – and despite the earlier intention, the price actually rose a little.

I am insufficiently artistic to describe the different stylistic nuances of the Chimaera against the Griffith, except to suggest that the Chimaera was meant to be a fast, relatively civilized, touring sportscar, whereas the Griffith was undoubtedly a red-blooded, aggressively-charactered Supercar. It showed in the way the cars handled, were equipped and the noise they made. The Griffith, in a way, was a slightly tamed wild animal; the Chimaera was domesticated from Day One.

Like the Griffith, the new car used the same chassis, suspension, TVR Power/Rover V8 engine and Rover-based five-speed transmission, along with the same Ford Sierra/Scorpio rear axle, but it was redeveloped in many minor details. From the start the engine was fitted with catalysts as standard equipment, the primaries taking a lot of space near the front of the engine bay.

Although the wheel/tyre combination was the same as on the 1992 Griffith, compared with that car the suspension settings had been softened a little, Bilstein dampers had taken the place of Konis, and an anti-roll bar was fitted at the rear. When Griffith rear-end grip and roadholding were being criticized in 1992, TVR were reluctant to fit a rear anti-roll

Legend has it that some details of the Chimaera's nose were influenced by a bite which Peter Wheeler's gundog took out of the foam mock-up shell! The Chimaera was similar to the Griffith in many ways, but almost every detail was different. Sales began in 1993, when it became TVR's best-seller. *(TVR)*

bar to alleviate the problem, but for the Chimaera there had been a change of policy.

As with the Griffith there was a choice of V8 engines with the familiar ratings – 3.95-litre/240bhp or 4.3-litre/280bhp. Visually these engines looked the same, except that the plenum chambers carried a '400' or '430' logo.

The major difference was in the styling, though at first (casual) glance the Chimaera might have come from a modified Griffith mould. Not so. Whimsically, perhaps, Wheeler and Ravenscroft agreed on a new project code – UP1, or Ugly Pig No 1 – and produced a rather different shape of car. Although the wheelbase and track dimensions, along with the wheels and tyres, were the same, and the bodyshell shared the same bulkhead, much of the floorpan and some other inner mouldings, the skin itself was different in every detail. Factory-provided figures show that the new

Chimaera was 2in longer than the Griffith, most of this extra length being at the rear where the boot was noticeably larger and deeper from front to rear.

In particular the Chimaera had new and very noticeable sill mouldings under the flanks, and bumper mouldings at front and rear; these made the overall aspect, from any angle, look rather less smooth and purposeful than the Griffith. At the rear the tail-lamp treatment was new and there was a definite lip above the rear number-plate. At the front of the car the Chimaera's headlamps were exposed (those of the Griffith were under transparent fairings), there was a larger air intake – this, no doubt, had something to do with the need to keep the catalysts cool – and there were no driving lamps. A pair of oddly-profiled recesses surrounded the turn indicators; TVR legend has it that Peter Wheeler's gundog, Ned, took a bite out of this corner of the original foam mock-up for the car, and Wheeler liked the effect so much that he retained it in the final style!

At the time of the Chimaera's launch, Peter Wheeler confirmed that it was John Ravenscroft and himself who inspired the shapes by carving out blocks of foam until the required shape had been achieved: "It's all pure sculpture. You won't see a CAD system around here...".

As on the Griffith, there was a one-piece removable panel over the seats as part of the 'soft top', and the doors were moulded inboard of the front wings at their leading edges, but there was a different type of latch release, and on the Chimaera the bonnet was hinged at the absolute front of the shell. The bonnet moulding had two vents, one on each side and close to the edges; these might have produced more airflow through the engine bay, but they were mainly present as styling features.

Inside the car there were similarities in layout, but many changes in detail, noticeably on and around the transmission tunnel, where a rotatable aluminium knob actuated the interior door releases.

The Chimaera made its bow at the NEC, as hoped, and for once a new TVR model was almost ready to go into production. Assembly of the first cars began soon after the New Year in 1993, 40 of them being completed in February, no fewer than 60 in March, and a further 56 in April. This was the period during which Griffith production for the UK market had ceased and export-market production had almost dried up and, seemingly almost without trauma, another best-selling TVR had been put on to the market.

Peter Wheeler's strategy had been to make the Chimaera just that important bit more 'touring' than the Griffith, yet to sell it at a similar price. A quick look at these late-1992 UK retail prices shows that he succeeded:

Griffith (4-litre, 240bhp)	£24,802
Griffith (4.3-litre, 280bhp)	£27,206
Chimaera (4-litre, 240bhp)	£25,200
Chimaera (4.3-litre, 280bhp)	£28,320

Once the motoring press got their hands on a car – *Fast Lane* in time for May 1993 publication and *Autocar & Motor*

Compared with the Griffith, the Chimaera had a pronounced sill moulding on the flanks, and what looked like a rear bumper moulding around the tail. The tail lamp treatment was also different – but the performance was just as exciting! (TVR)

97

in June – TVR was relieved to note a favourable impression.

Fast Lane used a 240bhp/3.95-litre example and recorded an astonishing 4.7sec for the 0–60mph sprint, with 0–100mph coming up in 12.1sec, and a top speed of 152.6mph achieved at the Millbrook test track: "It is an outstandingly good sports car, and few cars with fancy names, at double or treble the price, offer any competition to its performance… It's plenty of car for the money… Nobody else sells cars with this level of performance at such bargain prices. No wonder there is a waiting list; it's surprising there aren't riots… Overall, this is possibly the best-handling front-engined/rear-driven sports car in the world. At this price nothing else comes close."

Autocar & Motor carried out two jobs at once, not only by driving the 4-litre/240bhp Chimaera – a different test car, by the way – but by comparing it, head-to-head, with the new MG RV8. After studying the results of this twin-test, Rover publicists must have wondered what hit them. As the testers noted: "Conceptually, both cars speak the same language… they are both two-seat, rear-drive convertibles, marketed as sports tourers rather than outright sports cars… The Chimaera holds a sizeable performance advantage here. A power-to-weight ratio of 234bhp per tonne is successfully translated into stunning acceleration times that, give or take a few tenths, are in touch with those recorded by the fearsome Griffith 4.3. Zero to 60mph from standstill comes up in only 5.2sec and 100mph in 13.2sec." In this case the quoted top speed was 158mph.

"All this is carried off with the typical TVR hallmarks of a powder-keg exhaust note, meaty gearshift and weighty clutch action… Best news is the ride quality, which is a sight more absorbent than the Griffith's without losing the firmness necessary for a sports car.

The Chimaera's facia and control layout was similar to that of the Griffith, but with many different details, especially on and around the transmission tunnel. *(TVR)*

One of the first Chimaera chassis being assembled in 1993. The close similarity to the Griffith is clear. Note, too, that TVR now makes (and proudly placards) its own steering rack assembly. *(TVR)*

"And a sporting car the Chimaera is. Purists will call it a softened-up Griffith but it still feels like a man-sized sports car, positively raw next to the altogether more softly sprung MG... If it's not abundantly clear already, the newest TVR not only has the MG RV8 beaten hands down in virtually every dynamic area, it also has a far bigger boot, a wider, more spacious cabin, and creates a lot less wind noise."

After listing the Chimaera's fittings and specification, this review ended with the words: "How many more reasons do you need? None, as far as we can see."

The situation in mid-1993, therefore, was that the Chimaera had taken over smoothly where the Griffith had left off in 1992, the re-engined Griffith was about to re-enter the fray, and an all-new TVR engine was in the wings.

That engine, no question, was such an important project that it was set to make – or break – TVR's reputation in the next few years.

The AJP project

When TVR unveiled the prototype AJP8 engine in October 1992, they were at pains to stress that much more would be involved, for this was: "the generic prefix to all the products and developments that will emerge from this new high-tech research/development and manufacturing facility. The intention of AJP will be to design and manufacture engineering components, predominantly drivetrain related, to serve the TVR main production car division, and also fill the void that has always existed in the Motor Industry between the mass-produced component and the very expensive specialist single unit run."

These fine words confirmed that Peter Wheeler had struck up a close relationship with Al Melling, a Rochdale-based engine designer who claimed secret involvement in several important race-engine projects of the Eighties. As Wheeler said, in a 1992 interview: "I had said in the past that our

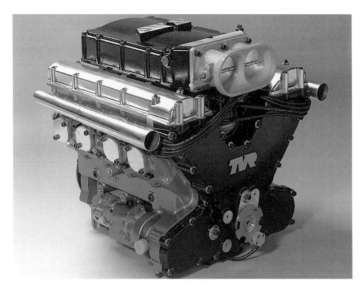

The prototype 4.2-litre AJP8 V8 engine had a vee-angle of 75 degrees and a claimed power output of 363bhp. It was shown at the 1992 NEC motor show and was originally intended for fitment into the Griffith, but development was prolonged; the Griffith was eventually relaunched with a 5-litre TVR/Rover V8 engine. The AJP engine, as shown here, had a two-valve, single-overhead cam layout, though other derivatives were possible. *(TVR)*

ultimate objective might be to get production up to 2,000 units a year, but it started to dawn on me that this was a very tall order, given that we've just had a fantastic year and sold about 1,000 cars. I started to think about other ways of expanding without going into businesses that needed heavy investment in promotion.

"Then I met Al in 1990. He had a hell of a pedigree, but seemed to be hiding his light under a bushel. We liked one another straight away and more or less cooked the whole idea up together."

The 'whole idea' included the Chimaera steering rack, which was the first AJP component to be used in the production cars, but the major long-term project was for Melling to design a new engine. This, of course, was a colossal undertaking, something which no other independent car maker had dared to attempt for a long time.

The first time I wrote it down, I was unhappy about that last remark, but a double-check into the archive shows that *every* British production car sold in recent years has either used a modified mass-production engine from one of the world's mass-market manufacturers, or has bought in its engines from Lotus, as did Jensen for the Jensen-Healey, or Cosworth – whose YB-Series turbocharged Ford Sierra Cosworth engine was used in several machines.

When the AJP8 engine was conceived, Peter Wheeler judged that the much-modified Rover V8 engine used in existing TVR models was reaching the limit of its development, at least as a flexible road-car unit. By 1993, that opinion may have had to be modified, for the Griffith 500's 5-litre unit provided a sturdy 325bhp which gave the latest model a stunning performance.

The AJP8, as previewed in 1992, was an ambitious design, and was apparently the first of a series of modular layouts. Melling claimed to have considered four or five additional derivatives, including a compact V12. Owing nothing to any other unit – it was *not*, as some people suggested, based on the Rover's existing cylinder block – it could not be, as the V8 was a 75-degree unit (so, incidentally, was Cosworth's famous racing HB V8), and it was immediately meant to produce more power than the Rover V8 had ever done. Initially it was postulated as a 4.2-litre engine producing 350/360bhp –

there were simpler alloy cylinder heads, with a single overhead camshaft layout and only two valves per cylinder. Naturally, his new AJP8 engine had an alloy cylinder block and cylinder heads, but it was also dry-sumped, very compact, and was claimed to weigh a mere 150kg/330lb.

When the prototype engine appeared at the motor show in October 1992 it had yet to run. It had taken eight months to make – from concept to completion of the mock-up – and at the time TVR claimed that it would go into production, for use in a modified Griffith, in March/April 1993. Seasoned motor industry pundits, who understood the complexities of emissions regulations, noise rules and other type approval matters, thought this was highly unlikely, but Peter Wheeler, as usual, merely smiled behind his moustache and commented: "Everything here is done quickly."

Nicely packaged, smaller than the TVR/Rover V8 engine and highly promising when launched in 1992, the AJP8 engine was originally expected to go into production in 1993. *(TVR)*

which compared well with the Griffith's 4.3 litres and 280bhp, or the 4.45-litre/320bhp engine used in the old 450SE.

Melling, whose past was rather mysterious and little chronicled – shrouded, he said, because of confidentiality clauses with his clients – had never worked in the cradle of engine design, Cosworth, where most great engine designers seem to learn their craft, but had apparently tried to sell the Northampton company several ideas in the past. His new engine was different, to say the least.

Not for him the conventional Nineties' solution of twin overhead camshafts and four valves per cylinder – though he said these had been investigated at the layout stage. Instead

Changing times. The modern Chimaera engine bay seems to find as much space for exhaust system catalysts as it does for the V8 engine itself. *(TVR)*

Space, but luxuriously trimmed space, for only two people in the cockpit of the 1993 Chimaera model. The bulky transmission tunnel also hides the multi-tube chassis-frame. *(TVR)*

This is a direct comparison between the AJP8 and the nearest equivalent TVR-Rover:

Detail	AJP8	TVR-Rover
Capacity	4,186cc	4,280cc
Vee angle	75deg	90deg
Bore x stroke	88 x 86mm	94 x 77mm
Compression ratio	Not quoted	10.0:1
Valve gear	Single overhead camshaft, two valves per cylinder	Overhead valve gear, pushrods and rockers, two valves per cylinder
Max power	363bhp at 7,000rpm	280bhp at 5,500rpm
Max torque	348lb.ft at 4,500rpm	305lb.ft at 4,000rpm

In 1993, however, TVR rapidly discovered that it would take much longer to get the AJP8 engine *ready* for production, let alone *in* production, than had been forecast. When I visited the factory in the summer of 1993, at a time when engine build should have begun, prototype testing was dragging on. In an embarrassing climbdown, TVR then had to keep the engine under wraps, for further development, and to fill the gap the 5-litre-engined Griffith 500 was rushed into the showrooms instead.

Would the promise of the AJP project be fulfilled? TVR enthusiasts would have to wait until 1994 to find out.

The hind quarters of the Chimaera were slightly humped – there was even a suggestion of AC Cobra in those lines – and the lip at the tail of the bootlid area made this car totally different in detail from the Griffith. *(TVR)*

CHAPTER 8

Projects and prototypes

Why were these not produced?

TVR have always been passionate about cars – new cars, fast cars, audaciously different cars. The people who work at the Blackpool factory are never happier than when playing with grown-up toys. Construction kits for children could usually be contained in one box – but at TVR, for grown men, they are usually large enough to be kept in one room.

At TVR, building cars to sell was one thing, but playing about with cars and developing prototypes – well, that was always much more exciting. It helped, of course, to have a proprietor who was a self-confessed 'car nut'. In the Eighties and Nineties, certainly, I could always visualize Peter Wheeler – and his gundog, Ned – getting rid of his day-to-day chores as soon as possible, leaving the mainstream business to his staff and sidling off to his development department where yet another new concept was brewing.

When most car-makers were struggling to stay alive, never mind having time to enjoy themselves, TVR – and Peter Wheeler – could always find the time to dabble. The company was small enough – and flexible enough – to take instant action, and to build prototypes in a matter of weeks.

Large firms would employ entire departments to spend months crunching numbers, talking to their dealers and spying on the opposition, but at TVR things happened quickly. Personalities like Peter Wheeler and Stewart Halstead would share a few pints, flick through a few magazines, and start something new: "Just suppose we chose *this* engine and slotted it into *that* chassis...but what axle would we use? ...how would it be if we restyled *that* body? How long would it take to make new moulds for...?"

To quote fellow-historian Mark Hughes, from his collected thoughts on TVR: "The Blackpool-based company takes a uniquely pragmatic approach to developing new models. Other manufacturers devote several years to preparing new cars in a cocoon of secrecy, trying to avoid the press gamesmanship of scoop pictures and leaked information prior to a public launch. When TVR has an idea for a new car, however, it knocks up a hand-made one-off, slips it on to a motor show stand, and waits for the reaction. If the response is strong enough, TVR will go into production, perhaps within a few months."

Once the Tasmin was launched and the decision taken to make derivatives of the design for some years to follow, there was time to start experimenting again. Over the years TVR started a large number of projects, some being abandoned at the testing stage, some being exhibited at motor shows as opinion-testers, but never taken further, while others inspired great production cars like the Griffith of the Nineties.

Every one of these cars, in one way or another, had an influence on the TVRs which were actually put on sale. It is unlikely that TVR have opened up every store cupboard for me to inspect, but the following were the most interesting 'might-have-been' models produced during the period:

Tasmin Turbo (1981 and 1982)
The star of TVR's motor show display at the NEC in October 1982 was the Tasmin Turbo prototype, which had not only much more horsepower than the series-production Tasmin, but also significantly modified styling. It was actually the

The 1982 TVR Turbo had its single turbocharger mounted high up on the left side of the engine – all that pipework leads round through an intercooler in the nose to the usual type of Ford V6 inlet manifold plenum chamber. Only two such cars were ever built. *(TVR)*

second such car to be produced – the first had been a Tasmin drophead, built in 1981 – but was quite undeveloped when put on display in Birmingham. Clearly it had been inspired by the Seventies-style Turbo, but as Stewart Halstead commented: "The new Turbo is a more practical car than the previous one. If we can develop a Drophead Turbo, I'd like to think that 40 or 50 a year are possible."

The turbocharged 2.8-litre Ford V6 engine had been developed 'in house', and was rated at 228bhp at 5,600rpm, with a peak torque figure of 249lb.ft at 3,200rpm – in other words, it was slightly less muscular than the Seventies-style 3-litre Turbo – and there was a five-speed gearbox, larger and more effective brakes and 16in wheels with wider-section tyres to keep things in check.

The styling featured an extended 'shovel-nose' with recessed driving lamps and a modified tail which included an integral spoiler. Initially, production was promised to start in March 1983, and the projected price was £16,800, which compared with £13,824 asked for the normally-aspirated model.

By 1983, however, everything had changed. Peter Wheeler had inspired the development of the Rover V8-engined 350i, which was a more practical, easier-to-build, Supercar, and it was that design which went into production instead. The two turbocharged cars were sold off – the drophead to John Britten Sports Cars and the silver coupe to Harrogate Horseless Carriages, and one can only speculate on their current whereabouts.

420 Sports Saloon (1986)

The problem with the original Tasmin +2 package was that there was really no usable occasional rear seat space, so

From the rear, TVR wanted to be sure that everyone realized that the Turbo *was* a Turbo... *(TVR)*

For the prototype Tasmin Turbo of 1982, TVR produced this modified style, with sharper-edged nose and different details. *(TVR)*

106

Shown as an undeveloped prototype at the 1986 NEC motor show was this new-generation 2+2 model, which TVR called the 420 Sports Saloon. It was claimed to have a far more useful '+2' accommodation than the obsolete Tasmin +2 Coupe. *(TVR)*

although sales and production of the +2 models died away in the mid-Eighties, Stewart Halstead and Peter Wheeler continued to believe in the potential of a more practical 2+2 model, and it was just such a car which was shown in October 1986.

The basic chassis was the same as that of the 420SEAC, but for this car an automatic self-levelling device was fitted at the rear. The engine, although the same 4,228cc size as that of the 420SEAC, ran in a slightly 'softer' tune, with a peak power output of 265bhp.

Most of the development work went into the evolution of a new (GRP composite) body, and although this included some basic inner panels from existing TVRs, it had a completely new exterior style and proportions. The nose was different from both the existing 350i *and* the new 420SEAC, the door apertures were also quite different, as was the tail, and there was a distinctive and rather angular fixed-head passenger cabin. The whole car was 8in longer than the current 350i Convertible, and TVR claimed that the rear seats were 'comfortable for two adults'.

In October 1986, the 420 Sports Saloon was priced at £24,500. though not, at that time, ready to go on sale.

Frankly, this car was not seen to be sufficiently attractive to

have a future, and there was little demand for it when it was exhibited at the NEC motor show. Before it was unveiled, I had seen it being shaped in TVR's development workshops, where inspiration was coming from a variety of sources.

There seemed to be all manner of influences, which resulted in angular cabin lines sitting uneasily behind a rounded nose. After the motor show it was never seen again, though it seems that at one time TVR proposed to clean up the lines, make it even longer than before and try again, though nothing came of this. They say that Peter Wheeler himself came to dislike it too…

Two years later there were second thoughts about a saloon model, for at the 1988 Paris show Peter Wheeler said that he aimed to introduce a £30,000 model in small numbers by mid-1989: "It will be neither a coupe nor a saloon, but it will give the family man a chance to own a TVR again."

It was also suggested that it would be powered by an all-new engine, though this did not appear for some years. Was this the original thinking behind the AJP8 unit?

ES Roadster (1987)

Only a year after the S model had been launched – and only weeks after deliveries had begun in the summer of 1987 –

The ES model appeared at the 1987 Motorfair exhibition and was meant to be the first of an evolutionary breed of S models. Various engines were mooted, one being a 3.8-litre Holden/GM V6 unit. Only one such car was ever produced. *(TVR)*

TVR chose the Motorfair exhibition of October 1987 to preview a development which was called the ES or HPS – depending on which TVR spokesman was talking about it at the time!

'E' apparently stood for Evolution (ES appeared as badging on the show car), and 'HP' for High Performance, which really meant that TVR was considering the use of different engines to take over from the Ford-Cologne V6 which powered the current S model.

Even at the time that Peter Wheeler took total control of TVR (May 1987), the company stated that it was about to start testing a competition version of the S, powered by a 350bhp version of the Ford Sierra Cosworth 2-litre engine, and the rumour-mongers suggested that a 205bhp road car would follow.

Such a road-car prototype was shown in October 1987,

with a projected price tag of £20,000, though even by that time other engines were being considered; there was no engine in the show car, which perhaps proves how undecided the company remained.

The Motorfair car featured modified front and rear suspension, a viscous-coupling limited-slip differential, and split-rim alloy wheels shod by 225/50VR-section Bridgestone tyres. Visually, there were modifications to the nose, with built-in auxiliary lamps and vents for the oil cooler.

The race car was a wild and ambitious machine, for it was very different from the NEC show car, having a rear-mounted axle/gearbox unit lifted straight out of a mid-engined race car, inboard disc brakes instead of the outboard drums of the road car, all allied to Rose-jointed double-wishbone rear suspension.

Suggestions that a V6-engined car complete with Sierra

XR4x4-type four-wheel drive might also be used can certainly be discounted, if only because I had recently lost a spirited argument with Wheeler and Halstead in which I had advocated four-wheel drive, and they had said they would *never* design a four-wheel-drive machine! In view of the way Panther later fell flat on its face with the Solo, maybe they were wise.

For commercial purposes two more engines were also being considered: one project was to use a slightly larger version of the existing 2.8-litre Ford-Cologne V6, which could produce more power and torque. TVR had the capability to make such changes without involving an engine builder, and actually showed a 3.2-litre V6 on the stand at Motorfair. This, though, was either misguided enterprise or a smokescreen to divert attention, for in the tuning business this engine was known to have inefficient cylinder heads and poor breathing, and in any case Ford was about to render it obsolete in favour of the 2.9-litre unit, which had better – though still not sensational – breathing capabilities.

Much more serious, and at the time very mysterious indeed, was the suggestion that "a new all-alloy 3.3-litre V6 from a major engine manufacturer" might also be used. At the

Head-on view of the 420 Sports Saloon of 1986. No-one seemed to like the styling – least of all Peter Wheeler himself! *(TVR)*

time TVR were extremely tight-lipped about this possibility, though it soon became clear that the engine was to be built by Holden of Australia for use in the Commodore VP. GM-Holden were certainly not about to admit that a 3.8-litre version of the new engine would also be available soon.

Peter Wheeler held high hopes of this engine, but in the end he was frustrated by General Motors' (especially Holden's) reluctance to take him seriously – reminiscent of the way Rover had to struggle to convince GM that *they* were serious when trying to buy the design rights for the alloy V8 in the Sixties... Promised prototype engines never turned up for installation, and finally he was forced to turn elsewhere.

This was a great pity. The all-new 'Holden' 90-degree V6, which carried the family name 'LN', was actually a GM-North America design but built in Australia at a Holden factory, and was scheduled to be fitted to a whole range of GM cars – held great promise. Although it was not technically advanced – it had pushrod overhead-valve gear and a single camshaft nestling in the centre off the vee – it had alloy cylinder heads *and* block and was meant to be installed either transversely (in front-wheel-drive GM cars) or in a traditional 'north-south' location – which would have suited TVR admirably.

This engine featured in several 1987 GM-North America models in a variety of cubic capacities and finally made its debut in the Holden Commodore in October 1988 (as a 170bhp 3.8-litre unit). Like the Rover V8 which TVR have used for so long, and in so many different guises, the GM-Holden V6 turned up in a number of different cars.

By 1993, when this book was being drafted, I traced LNs into six Buicks, one Chevrolet, the Holden VP, five Oldsmobiles and three Pontiacs! The 3.3-litre engine produced 162bhp and the most powerful 3.8-litre version no less than 203bhp when fitted with a Roots/Eaton type of supercharger.

Holden V8-engined hatchback (1986)

By the mid-Eighties TVR were beginning to think that time was running out for the versatile Rover V8 engine. Increasingly more time was having to be spent on tailoring it to the world's ever-tightening exhaust emission regulations. The

The original Speed Eight of 1989 was a two-seater model, intended as a replacement for the long-running 280i/350i/390SE Convertible. TVR only built one car, took it away for a rethink, and... *(TVR)*

Swedish and Swiss markets – both small, but significant – were the first to be abandoned, and Peter Wheeler could see more problems looming over the horizon.

His first idea was to revert to the 'Griffith' idea of the Sixties – where a lightweight Ford-USA V8 engine would be shoehorned into the TVR chassis. With that in mind, he asked his North American distributors to ship over a current Ford Mustang V8 unit – cast-iron block and cylinders, 4,942cc and about 225bhp with fuel injection – for trial, but it was simply too heavy and had to be abandoned.

This was the point at which General Motors-Holden of Australia approached him – discussions about the V6 engine already described came later – to see if he was interested in using their 5-litre V8, which had aluminium castings, and for which they claimed up to 250bhp in clean-exhaust guise.

This was a relative of the GM-North America V8s used in current Chevrolet Corvettes, and there was no doubt that the power *was* available. Holden Commodores intended for Australian Group A racing used this engine – 241bhp at

5,200rpm in road-car form – and it was strong and totally docile.

To assess it, Peter Wheeler had his engineers build a one-off for him to drive, the car being completed in October 1986. It was based on a 350i Coupe, with some 420SEAC features added below the belt-line; there was a new and sharp-edged nose with headlamps under Perspex covers, and the hatchback area was modified to provide a carpeted area for his dogs...

The Holden V8 engine slotted into place easily – it was a similar bulk to the well-known Rover V8 – and, as expected, it was as docile, flexible and satisfying as the Rover engine which it displaced.

The urgency fell out of the situation when TVR discovered that they could continue to make their modified Rover engines meet the regulations, so Peter Wheeler's one-off car, registered F120 SCK, never proceeded any further. John Barker of *Autocar & Motor*, who drove this car, wrote: "...the Holden engine lugs heartily from low revs and delivers its

...tried again at the 1990 NEC motor show with a longer 2+2 Speed Eight. Unhappily the prototype Griffith appeared at the same show, took so much attention – and so many orders – that the Speed Eight had to be abandoned. By the early Nineties it seemed to be too late to revive it. *(TVR)*

considerable mid-range thrust with a slightly unrefined but delicious burbling howl. From there to the 5,500rpm rev-limiter its beat to beat throb levels to a smooth, frenetic wail. Pure V8. It's not as polished as the Rover, but its honest characterful note is appealing."

Tuscan road car (1988)

The development of the late-Eighties Tuscan model has already been mentioned in Chapter 5. To summarize, Peter Wheeler conceived a new two-seater to become his ultimate-specification road car of the period and launched a value-for-money TVR Tuscan Challenge race series to publicize it.

During the winter of 1988–89, however, TVR's priorities changed, the new S *and* the old-type 350i/400SE/450SE models continued to keep the production lines very busy indeed, and the road-car version of the design, which would have utilized a 3.5-litre/225bhp version of the Rover-based V8 engine, was dropped.

In the end the chassis of the Tuscan was used as the basis of the Griffith (on sale in 1992) and the Chimaera (1993), so the development work was not wasted...

Speed Eight (1989 and 1990)

This was almost a classic case of TVR's famous 'suck-it-and-see' policy, for a one-off two-seater car shown at the London-based Motorfair of 1989 was followed by a further one-off development of the car, this time a version with a roomier cockpit and 2+2 seating, at the NEC motor show in October 1990. After that, nothing was ever heard of the car, and two years later the 2+2 could still be found, stored, dusty and neglected, at Blackpool.

In the beginning TVR set out to develop a straightforward and more rounded replacement for the successful Rover-engined 350i models, whose early-Eighties styling was beginning to look rather sharp-edged to be fashionable any more. The chassis layout was basically unchanged from the 350i, though it was given a 2in longer wheelbase – at 8ft this made it the longest-wheelbase TVR so far unveiled – and 4in wider wheel tracks, most of the suspension components being different from before.

The engine was a 225bhp 3.9-litre fuel-injected version of the famous Rover V8 unit, a considerably less powerful version of that sold in 390i models since 1984, and therefore likely to be totally and utterly reliable over a big mileage. Also, the shell/chassis-frame was engineered to allow bulky exhaust catalysts to be fitted if necessary.

The style, according to Wheeler, was "a more rounded version of the Tasmin wedge shape", which was certainly true, but the result was that it did not look very startling. As on the Tasmin/350i model, the headlamps were hidden under flaps, but although the general proportions were not changed – the nose was a wedge and the tail was short and relatively bulky – the lines were altogether more curvaceous. Perhaps it was right for 1989, but no more than that, and TVR's promise to get it on sale early in 1990 at a price of £22,995 was never fulfilled.

That car, in fact, never appeared again, for a year later, at the NEC motor show of October 1990, *another* Speed Eight made its appearance, this being a little longer than before, with similar styling, but billed as a 2+2-seater. This time TVR noted a 6in longer wheelbase than normal, and proposed a choice of V8 engines – a 3.9-litre for £24,495 or a 4.3-litre model for £27,495. Once again the first production models were promised for January, but again this never happened.

Two years later, in mid-1992, Wheeler admitted that the development of the Griffith model, which hit the market with such *eclat* in the winter of 1991–92, meant that work on every other major innovation had had to be temporarily sidelined: "Our dealers have been asking for a four-seater convertible for years, but it's a big step for us. It would increase our market potential enormously, and I'm not sure we could cope with that. It's certainly the case that it's easier for us to make high-performance two-seaters than a four-seater, which would need to satisfy a Jaguar owner. So the Speed Eight might change dramatically as well."

There must be several projects which TVR have considered in recent years, but never previewed in public. Even today – *especially today* – I have no doubt that they are working on several new projects, for this is clearly not a hide-bound, inward-looking concern which never plans for the future. Someday, perhaps, we will learn of other cars which were designed but never shown in public, since not all of them can come to fruition.

CHAPTER 9

Buying an older model

Choice, examination and appraisal

The author's aim in this chapter is merely to offer advice – hopefully presented in a logical manner – to anyone who might be considering the purchase of a car of the type covered. Such a car may be quite old, will almost certainly have dropped out of production, and may have suffered neglect by one or more previous owners. There is, therefore, no foolproof way of offering advice which holds good for every car and every model considered. In the case of the TVR, advice is given as a result of experience amassed with various cars, new or not so new.

The first and probably most important piece of advice to anyone considering buying an older TVR is that they should get a good idea of the cars' character when they were new. Technical progress has been rapid in recent years, so it can be discouraging to try out a well-used Tasmin from the early Eighties and expect it to be as capable as a modern Griffith or Chimaera. It is necessary to know what a Tasmin was *always* like – and not expect miracles.

It is hoped, as a result of the many facts this book contains, that a good basic grounding will already have been gained by the reader. Much may also be derived from reprints or originals of the impartial and accurate road tests carried out by the more reliable British and North American motoring magazines. In that category would be included *Autocar*, *Motor* – both before and since their amalgamation – and *Autosport* from the UK, along with *Road & Track* and *Car and Driver* from North America. The British monthlies – *Thoroughbred & Classic Cars* and *Classic and Sportscar*, for example – will also provide a 'good read' and some background knowledge, but tend not to give as much statistical and performance data as the more 'technical' publications.

The next point to be emphasized in connection with TVRs is that the supply of some models is very limited. Although the onset of terminal corrosion should not yet be a problem, it is a fact that the cars are more than usually vulnerable to crash damage. Therefore, although TVRs should not have suffered structural collapse due to rusting – the glassfibre bodies cannot rust, though they can go brittle with old and rough use, while the multi-tubular frames have often proved to be remarkably durable and long-living – many may have been scrapped after a serious accident. Leaning a TVR against a lorry, or the scenery, sometimes leads to shredding of bodywork and serious distortion of the frame and, as a result, many cars – intrinsically not worth much at the time of the accident – were scrapped there and then.

TVR enthusiasts probably do not need reminding that the supply of modern TVRs is still quite limited, even in the UK where most sales were made. As an example, detail figures quoted in Appendix D show that a total of 3,723 cars of all types were built in the Eighties, of which 2,559 were sold in the UK.

TVR enthusiasts in the USA are in for a very thin time unless they journey to the UK to find a right-hand-drive example to take back home, for *total* Eighties' TVR exports were 1,164 cars, of which less than 600 went to the US market. Every one of these cars was fitted with a 2.8-litre Ford V6 engine. TVR never marketed Rover V8-engined cars in the USA, which means that American enthusiasts must work out their own way of taking such a car back home with them.

Anyone looking to buy a particular TVR model should study Appendix D carefully before making up their mind. It is all very well looking for a Tasmin +2 – but there were only 47 of them – and lovers of closed TVRs (they were becoming progressively rarer as the Eighties progressed) should remember that the breed had virtually become extinct by 1985.

Compared with the late Eighties, however, prices have since become more reasonable. Perhaps the 'investment' mania for collecting anything, and paying inflated prices for it, passed away with that decade, which means that asking prices for older TVRs should have returned to more sensible levels. As with almost any production car, therefore, you can expect values to continue to fall for at least the first 10 years or more before there is any sign of the collector's interest underpinning price levels.

It is now time to risk nominating the cars which appeal to me, and those which do not have the same attraction. What follows is obviously a *personal* opinion; it may not be yours (which means, of course, that some TVR sellers will be delighted to know it).

Even by the early Nineties, there were three basically different types of TVR production cars to be considered: Tasmin-family models; S types; Griffith/Chimaera models. Each type was so different from the others that there really is little comparison between them. Take three different Rover-engined varieties, for instance: a late-Eighties 400i is vastly different from the early-Nineties V8S, while a Griffith or Chimaera is *certainly* nothing like either of them.

Even so, it *is* possible to categorize the three types: the S models have a 'retro' style that many older-TVR owners will find attractive; V6-engined Tasmin-family models are for those who like a fast car with Eighties-fashionable and rather angular styling, while TVR Power/Rover-engined cars are for those who put performance ahead of everything else. The modern Griffith, in particular, is for those who would like a Ferrari but can't afford the insurance! However, as said, the reader may think differently...

As stated in the companion volume to this book, I prefer torque delivered in large lumps, and from low rpm. I like my TVRs to be ferociously fast, and certainly to have more performance than mass-produced rivals. Like most TVR followers, I am more enthusiastic about TVR/Rover V8-engined cars than about those with Ford V6 engines.

A few readers may feel alienated by my belief that there is little merit in buying a Tasmin 200 today. At the time it was on the market, a Tasmin 200 was much cheaper than the 2.8-litre-engined cars, but even this could not turn it into a best-seller. Compared with those early-Eighties V6-engined cars, the 200 had much less power, and a look at the claimed performance figures shows that today it would probably be blown off by most of the current fuel-injected hot hatchbacks. Some 200s, it is said, were re-engined in later life; for once, I approve of that.

I prefer a soft-top car to a closed coupe, as did most new-TVR customers once they were given the choice, not in order to be fashionable, but because the modern TVR's soft-top was such a practical installation. Most drivers who treat their TVRs as 'classic toys' prefer to drive them with the top down. However, if the weather is awful, a properly-preserved soft-top is windproof, waterproof *and* solid enough to allow the car to be driven at high speed without tearing apart. Few other manufacturers can match the workmanlike way a TVR has of being fully open when needed, or to have effectively a 'roll bar' and a rigid roof panel as an alternative.

As far as the Ford 'Cologne' V6-engined cars were concerned, the later 2.9-litre engines had noticeably more low and medium-speed torque than the 2.8-litre types, but in spite of the better peak power figures, neither was as lusty from low speeds as the old 3-litre 'Essex' engine. TVR enthusiasts considering a change from the M-Series chassis should give the Tasmin or the S a good trial, especially in reasonably heavy traffic, before signing the cheque. The difference in character, if not in outright capability, is considerable. Driving behind a stump-pulling 'Essex', and forgetting to change gear once or twice, is one thing, but the same treatment doesn't work as well with 'Cologne'-equipped cars.

It would be quite impossible to advise on the purchase of a particular car in print. However, it is worth pointing out that the oldest of the TVRs featured in this volume is now well over 10 years old. Even though all the cars should be reasonably corrosion-proof (the tubular frames seem to last for many years without becoming structurally defective, while the glassfibre bodies should be impervious to any sort of deterioration except that of becoming brittle in certain circumstances), they are all going to *feel* old and tired in due course, not least in the way the bodies fit together, repel the wind and rain and stay rigid and creak-free.

Restoring a TVR to its former – and proper – glory is not for the faint-hearted, but at least there should not be the heart-breaking task of getting rid of acres of rust, and there seems to be a ready supply of spare parts, large or small, and the expertise to go with them; the final chapter covers this aspect of preservation in more detail.

Even before buying, however, a thorough road test is essential. All TVRs – and the earlier models with the less rigid frames were worse in this respect than their successors – were vulnerable to the accident which distorted the chassis, but was not serious enough to write-off the car completely. Since it is difficult to straighten a multi-tubular frame absolutely correctly without a great deal of time spent on the job (and a jig), there are probably a number of TVRs running around where the alignment is not what it should be. One object of the road test, therefore, should be to assess the car's straight-running behaviour and its cornering abilities to right and left. Do not be too proud to demand to sit behind the car as it goes along, in a friend's car, so that its behaviour can be personally observed.

Incidentally, and this point is mentioned in other chapters, it is worth emphasizing that great difficulty may be experienced in finding an older TVR which has not been 'customized' or made non-standard in some respects. This is because the glassfibre bodies are so easily altered by relatively unskilled mechanics, at quite a low cost (such things could certainly not be tackled on a car having a pressed-steel or a hand-built bodyshell) and it may mean that 'your' car may have slots or scoops where none should exist, or standard air intakes or outlets modified or blanked-off altogether. The heartening point to be made is that you, like the previous owner, can also change the contours fairly easily to restore the originality.

If you are still not sure you can properly 'vet' a TVR for originality, acquaint yourself with a club member who knows about these matters. There is nothing quite as impressive as the special knowledge held by an active member of the appropriate one-make club. The TVR Car Club is no exception – they rank specialist historians among their membership.

Much will eventually depend on your need for spare parts for the car you have decided to buy, and the situation as regards maintenance and restoration – issues to which the last chapter in this book is devoted. However, on the subject of restoration, it is surely not necessary to emphasize that dealing with the refurbishment, alteration and substitution of glassfibre panelling is not an activity for the novice. At certain stages of the game there may be fire risks and at others there may be a danger of inhaling the fibres themselves. While I agree that it is probably the easiest material for the ill-equipped amateur to attempt to repair without investing in expensive equipment, you are urged to take all the proper precautions before doing so. Useful advice of this nature will be found in Dennis Foy's book *Automotive Glassfibre* (MRP).

CHAPTER 10

Maintenance and fellowship

The Club, spares and restoration

In some previous *Collector's Guides*, dealing with cars which may have been built in large quantities, but have long ago dropped out of production, it is often reported that the provision of spare parts and service expertise has been abandoned. However, at the time of writing every TVR model covered – starting with the Tasmin of 1980 – was still actively supported and serviced by a thriving TVR factory, with a very helpful attitude to spare parts supply. Better still, not only is there an active TVR Car Club – but its relations with the factory are close and cordial.

As has been pointed out in earlier chapters, during the Eighties and Nineties TVR claimed to make between 75 and 80 per cent of the components which went into each car. This, along with the fact that most other fittings were either sourced from major manufacturers or from large and long-established suppliers, means that parts supply should not be a problem for some years to come.

The major 'bought-in' items, sometimes much-modified by TVR before being fitted to new cars, were engines (Ford or Rover units), transmissions and final-drive units. However, in the case of the Rover V8s, by the Nineties TVR Power had built up its business, and the engine capacities and power ratings had been pushed up so far that they were as much TVR as Rover.

In some instances – as with the Ford V6 engines and the earlier type of V8 engines fitted to the 350i – these were taken, virtually unmodified, from their manufacturers. It should be straightforward, therefore, to have them rejuvenated when the time comes. Even though the internals of a TVR Power V8 might be special to TVR, many of the basic components – especially the complex fuel injection systems – were not altered.

As far as 'fixtures and fittings' are concerned, all manner of proprietary items are also fitted. For the TVR owner who wants to do his own research, TVR supply Parts Manuals for all models. Everything listed therein has a TVR Part Number. However, it is surely not necessary to point out that a number of proprietary components – those designed for mass-production Austin-Rover, Ford and similar cars – have been used in TVRs over the years. More recently, however, TVR has moved gradually away from this policy; whereas you might have a happy time walking around an early Tasmin identifying door handles, tail-lamp clusters, steering wheels, switch gear, suspension components, brakes and other details, everything on a Griffith or a Chimaera is much more specialized.

Incidentally, if the owner cannot immediately identify something, he can be sure that the TVR parts supply specialists, and the TVR Car Club, have already done so!

The two largest TVR-sourced items are the bodyshells and the chassis frames. The good news here is that at the time of writing TVR had preserved all the appropriate jigs, tools and moulds, right back to the start of the Tasmin era, and kept up to date with demands for spares and repairs.

[As has already been made clear in Volume 1, in 1987 TVR sold off all of its pre-Tasmin parts, moulds and tooling to David Gerald TVR (of Worcestershire) in return for a promise to keep up the good work. This was great news for M

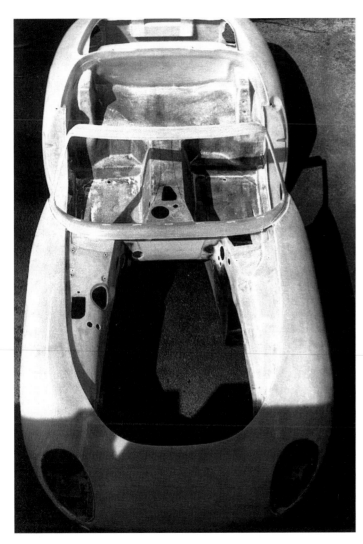

If you ever set out to restore a Griffith, this picture of the raw GRP shell may be useful! The joy of restoring any TVR is that the bodyshells are in very durable, rot-free, GRP, although even this material can deteriorate with age. *(TVR)*

and 3000S owners, but indirectly this also benefited owners of Eighties' and Nineties' TVRs, because it meant that henceforth the TVR factory could concentrate on their needs.]

Complete chassis-frames are either held in stock – by TVR or TVR dealers – or they can be made at relatively short notice. These are usually produced not only because they may be needed to straighten up a TVR after it has been crashed, but because there are now instances of multi-tubular frames which have become corroded after a lot of use in wet, muddy and particularly road-salty conditions.

TVR will not supply sections of the frame, nor provide drawings to allow an owner to make his own bodged repairs. It is probably fair to say that TVR would much prefer to supply completely new frames for repair or rebuilding purposes, as a frame which has once been crashed badly and perhaps 'straightened' by less than expert hands may never be the same again.

Similarly, the supply situation in regard to bodyshells, or removable sections such as doors, bonnet and bootlids, is encouraging. Because all TVRs have glassfibre bodies and, like other cars of this type, seem to suffer from 'corner' damage in shunts, a whole series of part-bodyshell sections have been made available from time to time. The owner or the dealer can work out how much of a shell is needed – or how much of an individual mould – and order replacements 'by the metre'! Complete bodyshells, too, have always been available.

In the case of body styling, be sure that any car you are considering buying today is original in every respect for its model and model year. Due to the gradual way in which the Tasmin evolved into the 350i, the 390SE and the 420SEAC during the Eighties, it is quite likely that a car may have been updated or modified by a previous owner and be something of a hybrid as far as originality fanatics are concerned.

Most older-car buyers like to see complete originality in their classic cars. In the case of older and once-neglected TVRs a car can always be returned to its as-manufactured state without too much practical difficulty – though it may not be at all cheap...

The supply of trim items may present problems – there was

such a wide choice of colours and patterns over the years – but with patience the restoration problems can be solved. Since TVR have made their own electrical wiring looms for a long time, the supply of new assemblies is feasible, and most electrical components are freely available. Examples are usually held in stock for the most numerous models.

In summary, unless money is a serious limiting factor, there is no reason why *any* TVR of this period, no matter how old or visually disreputable, should not be rebuilt to a thoroughly roadworthy condition. Once this has been done it should also be easy enough to make sure that it is properly maintained as the factory would recommend. Such chores are made easier by the fact that there is a great deal of factory-sourced or factory-approved literature available to cover the subject.

But how does a new TVR owner find out the provenance of his newly-acquired machine? One way to speed up the learning process is to meet other owners; almost certainly they will already be members of the TVR Car Club.

In the Eighties the TVR Car Club Ltd went through a series of financial traumas. However, in 1989 the Club became a limited company, at which point enthusiast Roger Cook stepped in as the Secretary, and by the Nineties it had developed into a thriving, apparently ever-expanding, organization; in 1993 Cook showed me just how far matters have progressed, most importantly by having put the services of his own company to operate as the office HQ:

TVR Car Club Ltd
(Roger Cook, Secretary)
21 Hawkeswood Road
Woodlands
Cheltenham
Gloucestershire
GL51 5DT

Tel: 0242-222878

Like most one-make clubs, the TVR Car Club seeks to provide spares and service for the cars, a forum for sales and wants – of cars and components – and leans more towards the preservation of the cars in the marque. Its atmosphere is closer to that of a social club than as a motorsport-orientated group.

Roger Cook, incidentally, is a typical one-make club fanatic, having owned three TVRs and been an enthusiast for the marque for many years. In 1959, the Club membership was about 1,250, but within four years it had risen to 3,000, and at the time of writing it was expanding fast. In the early Nineties, many buyers of new TVRs – S customers in particular – are joining the Club. Cook reckons that more than 40 per cent of members use their TVRs as 'toys' rather than as day-to-day working machines; at least one member is known to own six different cars!

Nor is Club membership exclusively British. While more than half *are* from the UK, there are also members in Europe (including Germany, Sweden and Switzerland), as well as Australia, Japan, New Zealand, Oman, Singapore – and more than 500 from the USA.

When this book was being prepared in 1993, the annual subscription to the Club was £25 (with a £5 joining fee for new members). Regular contact between the Club and its membership is assured by the publication of a very professional-looking magazine, *TVR Sprint*, which is published monthly.

Although the TVR factory has no stake in the Club, or any active part in the running of it, Chairman Peter Wheeler is also the President of the Club. This is really only a figurehead position; the principal contact with the factory comes through Roger Cook (from the Club), or from the factory through Brian Horner and Ben Samuelson.

"The relationship between the Club and the factory is as good as it has ever been," Roger Cook told me. "We are in touch the whole time, and we regularly get involved in publicity work, particularly if a dealer needs an older model to brighten up one of his displays. Basically, if we want anything *other* than money, TVR usually tries to provide it."

The largest TVR dealers – such as Barnet Motor Company (north of London), Team Central in Birmingham, Graypaul Motors and Harrogate Horseless Carriages – all support the Club's activities, sometimes slipping Club publicity leaflets into the glove pockets of cars going to new customers.

As far as the Club is concerned, in the UK it is split into 29

The TVR Car Club makes regular pilgrimages to the factory in Blackpool. This line of 3000Ms, Tasmins and Vixens was lined up outside the offices at an early-Eighties event. *(TVR)*

Regions, with almost every one getting together at least once a month. A mass visit to the factory is set up every other year, and the National Weekend is held annually at a different location. Track days at racing circuits also give owners a chance to unleash their TVRs in controlled conditions. Technical seminars, a meet usually concentrating on one particular subject, help enormously for those restoring the cars.

A recent development which, if other clubs' experiences are to be trusted, is bound to be a great incentive to joining the TVR Car Club is that a special insurance scheme is now operating in the UK. For the more modern TVRs, which tend to attract very high premiums from run-of-the-mill insurers, this is clearly a very important service.

Anyone with a TVR of this period should be able to keep his or her car in good condition by being a member of the TVR Car Club, and by keeping in touch with an established

TVR dealer. Even so, there may be occasions when contact with the factory is required.

TVR is a small concern with an informal organization, so there is no need to ask for a particular person. In particular, don't expect a personal reply from Peter Wheeler – he's far too busy! Their address is as follows:

TVR Engineering Ltd
Bristol Avenue
Blackpool
Lancashire
FY2 0JF

Telephone: 0253-56151
Fax: 0253-57105
Telex: 647519

TVR milestones – the important dates

To summarize the complex technical and commercial events which have taken place at TVR since the mid-Seventies, this Appendix should form a useful 'skeleton' around which the main story and the details can be filled in:

1947 Trevor Wilkinson formed TVR Engineering and built his first 'special'.

1958 Grantura Mark 1 put into series production. TVR Engineering dissolved. Layton Sports Cars Ltd formed to take its place.

1961 Beginning of the Aitchison-Hopton period of ownership. Layton Sports Cars Ltd formed to take its place.

1962 Announcement of Mark III coil-spring chassis and short-lived competitions programme. Trevor Wilkinson left the firm in April. Bankruptcy of TVR Cars Ltd in autumn. Grantura Engineering Ltd (a creditor of the bankrupt company and its main supplier) took up the manufacture of TVRs.

1965 Trident prototype revealed, but lost to other hands during the year. Collapse of Grantura Engineering in August. Purchase of all assets by Arthur and Martin Lilley in November. Formation of TVR Engineering Ltd.

1970 Assembly facilities moved from original Hoo Hill factory to the Bristol Avenue, Bispham, works – completed over the Christmas period.

1975 Serious disruption due to fire at Bristol Avenue on January 3, 1975. Production restarted in March/April. TVR Turbo (with Broadspeed-modified 3-litre Ford engine) announced at Earls Court motor show.

1976 Introduction of Taimar with hatchback.

1977 Last de-toxed 2500M built (for the USA) as engine taken out of production by Triumph. 3000M took its place.

1978 Introduction of TVR Convertible – first drophead series-production TVR, which instantly took over majority of TVR sales.

1979 Last M-Type/Taimar/Convertible models built prior to launch of all-new TVR in 1980.

1980 Launch, in January, of Tasmin – new chassis, new body style, new engine (German Ford, 2.8-litre V6 with fuel injection) – no carry-over of components, except in minor detail, from M-Type range. Two-seater Coupe at first, joined in October (at NEC motor show) by two-seater Convertible and 2+2 Coupe. Automatic transmission option announced at NEC motor show.

1981 S2 two-seater Coupe replaced original Tasmin Coupe. 2-litre Ford-engined Tasmin 200 announced.

1982 Peter Wheeler bought control from Martin Lilley; Stewart Halstead became Managing Director. Prototype Tasmin Turbo shown, but not put into production.

1983 Relaunch of TVR in the US market. Launch of Rover V8-engined 350i models. 'Tasmin' name dropped in favour of '280i' name.

1984 Launch of 390SE Convertible with 275bhp engine. Last Tasmin 200 built.

1985 280i became Series 2 in US market. 350i Convertible became Series 2 in all other markets. Last +2 models built. First 390SE built with optional 4.2-litre engine.

1986 Launch of two important new models – 420SEAC and S Convertible. 420 Sports Saloon shown, but never put on sale.

1987 Peter Wheeler took complete control of TVR by buying Stewart Halstead's shareholding. Series production of S model began. All pre-Tasmin jigs and parts sold to David Gerald TVR; henceforth TVR Blackpool concentrated on support of Eighties and Nineties models.

1988 New-generation Tuscan unveiled. Plans announced for Tuscan Challenge racing series. 450SEAC and 400SE deliveries began. Last Tasmin-shape V6-engined 280i model built.

1989 35 Tuscan race cars built and delivered, but road-car programme cancelled. 450SE added as top-of-the-range alternative to 350i. Last SEAC model – a 450SEAC – built. Two-seater Speed Eight unveiled, but not put on sale.

1990 Speed Eight 2+2 project unveiled, but again not put on sale. Griffith two-seater prototype (a non-runner) unveiled.
1991 Last Tasmin-shape model – a 400SE – built. V8S model put on sale.
1992 Griffith deliveries began in January, this model generating an enormous demand. Launch of new Chimaera model, using the Griffith chassis, but with a new style of convertible two-seater body. Deliveries began in early 1993. New AJP8 (V8) engine project revealed, with series production scheduled for 1993.
1993 Chimaera deliveries began. Griffith assembly run down to make way for Chimaera. AJP8 engine build delayed. New Cerbera 2+2 prototype revealed.

APPENDIX B
Technical specifications

Tasmin S1 (two-seater Coupe) – produced 1980 and 1981
Engine: German Ford unit, V6-cyl, 93 x 68.5mm, 2,792cc; CR 9.2:1, Bosch K-Jetronic fuel injection. 160bhp (DIN) at 5,700rpm. Maximum torque 162lb.ft at 4,300rpm.
Transmission: Ford all-synchromesh gearbox, or Ford automatic transmission. Axle ratio 3.07:1. Overall gear ratios (manual transmission) 3.07, 4.33, 5.96, 9.70, reverse 10.28:1. Overall gear ratios (automatic transmission) 3.07, 4.53, 7.60, reverse 6.48:1. 22.2mph/1,000rpm in top gear.
Suspension and brakes: Ifs, coil springs, wishbones, anti-roll bar, telescopic dampers. Irs, trailing links, transverse links, fixed-length driveshafts, combine coil spring/telescopic damper units. Rack-and-pinion steering. 10.6in front disc brakes, 10.9in rear discs, with vacuum-servo assistance. Bolt-on cast-alloy disc wheels with 7in rims. 205/60VR-14in tyres.
Dimensions: Wheelbase 7ft 10in; front track 4ft 8.5in; rear track 4ft 8.7in. Length 13ft 2in; width 5ft 8in; height 3ft 11in. Fuel tank 14galls. Unladen weight 2,365lb.
Basic price: £10,274 in spring 1980 with manual transmission, automatic transmission £400 (basic) extra. £11,096 from May 1981.

Tasmin S2 Coupe – produced 1981 to 1985
(Renamed 280i Coupe in 1983)
1981 specification, as for Tasmin S1 Coupe except for:
Length 13ft 5in. engine later re-rated by Ford to 150bhp (DIN) at 5,700rpm.
From October 1982: Optional Ford five-speed all-synchromesh gearbox, with axle ratio of 3.54:1. Overall gear ratios 2.90, 3.54, 4.53, 6.37, 11.89, reverse 11.91:1. 24.5mph/1,000rpm in top (5th) gear. Other options included automatic transmission, power-assisted steering and air conditioning.
Basic price: £12,855 from May 1986, total price £16,015.
Note: US-market version went on sale from spring 1984, with 145bhp at 5,700rpm, overall length 13ft 7in and unladen weight approx 2,700lb.

Tasmin Convertible – produced 1980 to 1988
(Renamed 280i Convertible in 1983)
1981 specification as for Tasmin Coupe except for convertible body style:
Length 13ft 2in. Engine later re-rated to 150bhp as S2 Coupe.
From October 1982: Optional Ford five-speed all-synchromesh gearbox, automatic transmission, power-assisted steering and air conditioning, details as Coupe S2.
Basic price: £12,200 from May 1986, total price £15,200.
Note: US-market version went on sale from spring 1983 with 145bhp at 5,700rpm and overall length of 13ft 4in. This car became Series 2 from spring 1985 with styling and equipment changes.

Tasmin +2 – produced 1981 to 1985
Specification and all updating changes as for Tasmin S2 Coupe except for +2 seating.
Basic price: £11,077 in autumn 1980, automatic transmission £400 (basic) extra. Last quoted price £12,690 in 1985.

Tasmin 200 Coupe – produced 1981 to 1984
Specification as for 2.8-litre Tasmin S2 Coupe except for:

Engine: Ford overhead-cam unit, 4-cyl, 90.8 x 76.95mm, 1,993cc, CR 9.2:1, twin-choke Weber carb, 101bhp (DIN) at 5,200rpm. Maximum torque 112lb.ft at 3,500rpm.
Transmission: Axle ratio 3.44:1. Overall gear ratios 3.44, 4.71, 6.78, 12.56, reverse 12.59:1. 19.1mph/1,000rpm in top gear. No automatic transmission option.
Suspension: 6in wheel rims, 195/60HR-14in tyres.
Dimensions: Unladen weight 2,138lb.
Basic price: £8,015 on announcement in December 1981.

Tasmin 200 Convertible – produced 1981 to 1984
Specification as for 2.8-litre Tasmin Convertible except for mechanical details as for 200 Coupe.
Basic price: £7,934 on announcement in December 1981.

350i Convertible – produced 1983 to 1985
Specification as for Tasmin/280i Convertible except for:
Engine: Rover overhead-valve unit, V8-cyl, 88.9 x 71.12mm, 3,528cc, CR 9.75:1, Lucas fuel injection. 190bhp (DIN) at 5,280rpm. Maximum torque 220lb.ft at 4,000rpm.
Transmission: Rover all-synchromesh gearbox, or GM automatic transmission. Axle ratio 3.54:1. Overall gear ratios (manual transmission) 2.80, 3.54, 4.96, 7.40, 11.75, reverse 12.14:1. 25.4mph/1,000rpm in top (5th) gear. Overall gear ratios (automatic transmission) 3.54, 5.24, 8.50, reverse 6.80. 20.1mph/1,000rpm in top gear.
Suspension: 7in wheel rims. 205/60VR-15in tyres.
Dimensions: Height 3ft 11.5in. Unladen weight 2,536lb.
Basic price: £11,880 on announcement in autumn 1983. Automatic transmission £417 (basic), power-assisted steering £265 (basic) and air conditioning for £534 (basic).

350i Convertible Series 2 – produced 1985 to 1990
Specification as for Series 1 model except for:
Engine: 197bhp (DIN) at 5,280rpm.
Basic price: £13,625 from May 1986.

350i Coupe – produced 1983 to 1990
Specification as for Tasmin/280i S2 Coupe except for mechanical details as for 350i Convertible.

350i +2 Coupe – produced 1983 and 1984
Specification as for Tasmin/280i +2 Coupe except for mechanical details as for 350i Convertible.

390SE Convertible – produced 1984 to 1988
Sold as an Option Package on 350i Convertible. Same specification except for:
Engine: 93.5 x 71.12mm, 3,905cc, CR 10.5:1, 275bhp (DIN) at 5,500rpm. Maximum torque 270lb.ft at 3,500rpm.
Transmission: Limited-slip differential standard. Note: Optional 3.07:1 axle ratio.
Suspension: 225/50VR-15in, later 225/60VR-15in, tyres.
Price: Always priced as a conversion on top of 350i prices. From May 1986 *total* extra UK cost was £3,810.
Note: To special customer order, a few cars were fitted with 4.2-litre engine, as to be used in 420SEAC model.
From April 1988: Flared sills, new bumpers, slimmer screen pillars. Larger ventilated disc brakes, 4-pot calipers, variable rate coil springs, adjustable gas-filled dampers and OZ 8in split-rim wheels, plus new instruments and improved heating/ventilation added to specification. Automatic transmission as an option was discontinued from *all* models in 1986.

400SE – produced 1988 to 1991
Specification as for 390SE except for:
Engine: Rover/TVR 94 x 71.12mm, CR 10.5:1, 3,948cc. 275bhp (DIN) at 5,500rpm. Maximum torque 270lb.ft at 3,500rpm.
Transmission: Axle ratio 3.31:1. Overall gear ratios 2.62, 3.31, 4.64, 6.92, 10.99, reverse 11.35:1. 28.5mph/1,000rpm in top gear. Optional 3.43 and 3.54:1 axle ratios.
Total price: £24,995 in 1988.

450SE – produced 1989 and 1990
Specification as for 390SE/400SE except for:
Engine: Rover/TVR 94 x 80mm, 4,441cc, CR 9.75:1. 320bhp at 5700rpm. Maximum torque 310lb.ft at 4,000rpm.
Transmission: Axle ratio 3.43:1. 28.5mph/1,000rpm.
Suspension: 225/50VR-15in tyres with 8.5in wheel rims, or optional 245/45VR-16in tyres on 9in rims.
Total price: £27,995 in 1989.

420SEAC – produced 1986 to 1988

Basic specification as for 350i Convertible family, but with body style changes and different body materials:

Engine: Rover/TVR overhead-valve unit, V8-cyl, 93.5 x 77mm, 4,228cc; CR 9.75:1, Lucas fuel injection. 300bhp (DIN) at 5,500rpm. Maximum torque 290lb.ft at 4,500rpm.

Transmission: Rover five-speed all-synchromesh manual gearbox. Axle ratio 3.54:1. Overall gear ratios 2.80, 3.54, 4.94, 7.39, 11.76, reverse 12.135:1. 24.6mph/1,000rpm in top gear. Optional 3.07:1 axle ratio, 28.5mph/1,000rpm in top gear.

Suspension and brakes: Ifs, coil springs, wishbones, anti-roll bar, telescopic dampers. Irs, coil springs, wishbones, anti-roll bar, telescopic dampers. Rack-and-pinion steering with power-assistance. 10.6in front disc brakes, 10.9in rear discs, with vacuum-servo assistance. Bolt-on cast-alloy disc wheels with 8.5in rims and 225/50VR-15in tyres; optional 9in rims and 245/45VR-16in tyres.

Dimensions: Unladen weight 2,492lb.

Total price: £29,500 in 1986.

450SEAC – produced 1988 and 1989

Specification as for 420SEAC, but with enlarged engine:

Engine: Rover/TVR, 94 x 80mm, 4,441cc, CR 9.75:1. 324bhp (DIN) at 5,700rpm. Maximum torque 310lb.ft at 4,000rpm.

Transmission: Axle ratio 3.43:1. 29.4mph/1,000rpm in top gear.

Total price: £33,950 in 1989.

S (retrospectively known as S1) – produced 1986 to 1988

Engine: German Ford unit, V6-cyl, 93 x 68.5mm, 2,792cc, CR 9.2:1, Bosch K-Jetronic fuel injection. 160bhp (DIN) at 6,000rpm. Maximum torque 162lb.ft at 4,300rpm.

Transmission: Ford all-synchromesh gearbox. Axle ratio 3.64:1. Overall gear ratios 2.98, 3.64, 4.59, 6.59, 12.23, reverse 12.25:1. 23.4mph/1,000rpm in top gear. Optional 3.36:1 axle ratio, 25.35mph/1,000rpm in top gear.

Suspension and brakes: Ifs, coil springs, wishbones, anti-roll bar, telescopic dampers. Irs, coil springs, semi-trailing arms, telescopic dampers. Rack-and-pinion steering. 9.4in front disc brakes, 9 x 2.25in rear drums, with vacuum-servo assistance. Bolt-on cast-alloy disc wheels with 7in rims. 205/60VR-15in tyres.

Dimensions: Wheelbase 7ft 6in; front track 4ft 7in; rear track 4ft 7in. Length 13ft; width 5ft 7in; height 4ft. Fuel tank 12 galls. Unladen weight 2,175lb.

Total price: £12,995 in 1987.

S2 – produced 1988 to 1991

Specification as for original S (S1) except for:

Engine: 93 x 72mm, 2,935cc, CR 9.5:1, Bosch L-Jetronic fuel injection. 170bhp (DIN) at 5,700rpm. Maximum torque 172lb.ft at 3,000rpm.

Total price: £15,450 in 1988.

S3, S3C and S4C – produced from 1990

Mechanical specification as for S2, but with longer doors and many trim/equipment improvements. S3 with same engine as S2, S3C with catalyst-equipped engine. Engines rated at 168bhp (DIN) at 5,400rpm; maximum torque 191lb.ft at 3,575rpm. S4C with 10.6in front discs brakes, 9.9in rear discs.

Total price: S3 £17,699 in 1990.
S3C £19,499 in 1990.

V8S – produced from 1991

Basic specification and layout based on that of V6-engined S3 model with this detail specification:

Engine: Rover/TVR overhead-valve unit, V8-cyl, 94 x 71 mm, 3,948cc, CR 10.5:1, Lucas fuel injection. 240bhp (DIN) at 5,750rpm. Maximum torque 275lb.ft at 4,200rpm.

Transmission: Rover all-synchromesh gearbox. Axle ratio 3.36:1. Overall gear ratios 2.65, 3.36, 4.69, 7.01, 11.16, reverse 11.52:1. 26.9mph/1,000rpm in top gear. Alternative 3.31, 3.43 and 3.54:1 axle ratios.

Suspension and brakes: Ifs, coil springs, wishbones, anti-roll bar, telescopic dampers. Irs, coil springs, semi-trailing arms, telescopic dampers. Rack-and-pinion steering. 10.6in front disc brakes, 9.9in rear discs, with vacuum-servo assistance. Bolt-on cast-alloy disc wheels with 6.5in rims. 205/60ZR-15in tyres.

Dimensions: Wheelbase 7ft 6in; front track 4ft 8.6in; rear track 4ft 8.6in. Length 13ft; width 5ft 5.5in; height 4ft. Fuel tank 12 galls. Unladen weight 2,247lb.

Total price: £23,595 in 1991.

Optional equipment included:

Engine: 88.9 x 40.25mm, 1,998cc, CR 8.4:1. Lucas fuel injection plus Eaton supercharger. 223bhp (DIN) at 6,200rpm. Maximum torque 196lb.ft at 3,700rpm.

Transmission: Ford all-synchromesh unit, with 3.64:1 axle ratio.

Tuscan – produced from 1989

(In this form used only for racing in TVR Tuscan Challenge.)

Engine: Rover/TVR overhead-valve unit, V8-cyl, 94 x 80mm, 4,441cc, CR 12:1, 4 twin-choke Weber carbs. In 1989, typically 400bhp (DIN) at 7,000rpm. Maximum torque 360lb.ft at 5,500rpm. More power and torque on further developed models.

Transmission: Borg-Warner all-synchromesh gearbox. Axle ratio 3.72:1. Overall gear ratios 2.98, 3.72, 4.98, 7.22, 10.97, reverse 10.25:1. 23.6mph/1,000rpm in top gear.

Suspension and brakes: Ifs, coil springs, wishbones, anti-roll bar, telescopic dampers. Irs, coil springs, wishbones, anti-roll bar, telescopic dampers. Rack-and-pinion steering. 11.8in front disc brakes, 11.6in rear discs, with vacuum-servo assistance. Bolt-on cast-alloy disc wheels with 9in rims. 210/60-16in Dunlop racing tyres.

Dimensions: Wheelbase 7ft 8in; front track 4ft 10.3in; rear track 4ft 10.3in. Length 12ft 11in; width 5ft 8.5in; height 3ft 8.5in. Fuel tank 12 galls. Unladen weight 2,240lb.

Griffith – produced 1991 to 1993

Engine: Rover/TVR overhead-valve unit, V8-cyl, 94 x 77mm, 4,280cc, CR 10:1, Lucas fuel injection. 280bhp (DIN) at 5,500rpm. Maximum torque 305lb.ft at 4,000rpm.
Alternative engine, 94 x 71.12mm, 3,948cc, CR 9.8:1. 240bhp (DIN) at 5,250rpm. Maximum torque 270lb.ft at 4,000rpm.

Transmission: Rover all-synchromesh gearbox. Axle ratio 3.31:1. Overall gear ratios 2.61, 3.31, 4.63, 6.92, 10.99, reverse 11.35:1. 27.04mph/1,000rpm in top gear.

Suspension and brakes: Ifs, coil springs, wishbones, anti-roll bar, telescopic dampers. Irs, coil springs, wishbones, telescopic dampers. Rack-and-pinion steering. 10.6in front disc brakes, 9.9in rear discs, with vacuum-servo assistance. Bolt-on cast-alloy disc wheels with (front) 7in rims, 205/55ZR-15in tyres; (rear) 7.5in rims, 225/50ZR-16in tyres.

Dimensions: Wheelbase 7ft 6in; front track 4ft 10in; rear track 4ft 10.4in. Length 13ft; width 6ft 1.4in; height 3ft 10.6in. Fuel tank 12.7 galls. Unladen weight 2,304lb.

Total price: (4-litre) £25,795 in 1992.
(4.3-litre) £28,295 in 1992.

Griffith 500 – produced from 1993

Specification as for original Griffith except for:

Engine: 94 x 90mm, 4,988cc; 325bhp (DIN) at 5,500rpm. Maximum torque 350lb.ft at 4,000rpm.

Suspension and brakes: Power-assisted steering optional. 10in front disc brakes, 10.5in rear discs.

Chimaera – produced from 1993

Engine: Rover/TVR overhead-valve unit, V8-cyl, 94 x 71.12mm, 3,948cc, CR 9.8:1, Lucas fuel injection. 240bhp (DIN) at 5,250rpm. Maximum torque 270lb.ft at 4,000rpm.
Alternative engine: 94 x 77mm, 4,280cc; CR 8.9:1. 280bhp (DIN) at 5,500rpm. Maximum torque 305lb.ft at 4,000rpm.

Transmission: Rover all-synchromesh gearbox. Axle ratio 3.31:1. Overall gear ratios 2.61, 3.31, 4.63, 6.92, 10.99, reverse 11.35:1. 27.04mph/1,000rpm in top gear.

Suspension and brakes: Ifs, coil springs, wishbones, anti-roll bar, telescopic dampers. Irs, coil springs, wishbones, telescopic dampers, anti-roll bar. Rack-and-pinion steering, optional power-assistance. 10.6in front disc brakes, 9.9in rear discs, with vacuum-servo assistance. Bolt-on cast-alloy disc wheels with (front) 7in rims, 215/50ZR-15in tyres; (rear) 7.5in rims, 225/50ZR-16in tyres.

Dimensions: Wheelbase 7ft 6in; front track 4ft 9.5in; rear track 4ft 9.5in. Length 13ft 2in; width 6ft 1.4in; height 4ft. Fuel tank 12.7 galls. Unladen weight 2,337lb.

Basic price: (4-litre) £26,250 in 1993.
(4.3-litre) £28,950 in 1993.

APPENDIX C

Chassis number sequences

A totally new sequence of chassis identification was adopted to distinguish the new Tasmin family when it was launched in 1980. Accordingly, there should never be any confusion with earlier TVR models:

Tasmin Coupe S1	1979 to 1981	Ford V6 2.8	FH5001FI to 5196FI
Tasmin Convertible	1980 onwards	Ford V6 2.8	DH5098FI onwards
Tasmin +2 Coupe	1980 onwards	Ford V6 2.8	FH5113F12 onwards
Tasmin Coupe S2	1981 onwards	Ford V6 2.8	FH5211FIT onwards
Tasmin 200s	1981 to 1984	Ford 2000	...2L suffix
350i/390SE	1983 onwards	Rover V8 3.5/3.9	...RI suffix

This Chassis Number sequence was abandoned, at DH6040FI, in March 1985. From that date, 'Euro-rationalized' Vehicle Identification Numbers (VIN Nos) were adopted. The first of the new-style VINs was:

TV9RF28P4FBDH1280RI

– where the last eight digits (DH1280RI) coincided with the old-style chassis sequence.

This sequence was changed from mid-1985 from:

SA9DH28PXFBO19433

Each of the digits means the following:

S} Made in the UK.
A} Less than 500 vehicles per annum.
9}

D} Description of body. DH = drophead, FH = fixedhead.

H} Weight class B (3,001–4,000lb GVW).

2} Engine size. 28 = Ford 2.8-litre
8}   35 = Rover 3.5-litre

P} Fuel.   P = Petrol or gasoline.

X} VIN Verification check digit.
F} Manufacturing year. F = 1985, G = 1986, H = 1987

B} Manufacturing plant. B = Blackpool.

0} International code, designating TVR 280i & 350i fixedhead &
1} drophead. TVR Engineering Limited, Bristol Avenue, Blackpool,
9} Lancs, FY2 0JF.

4}
3} Sequential build number.
3}

Notes:
1. Tasmin S2 Coupe numbering changed almost immediately after release. From Chassis Number 5232, a complete identification became 2FH5232FI.
2. An entirely new sequence was adopted for the Tasmin models. Numbers start at 5001. The prefix FH refers to a fixed-head car (2-seat or 2+2 seat), while DH refers to the drophead or Convertible Tasmin. The suffix FI refers to the fuel-injected Ford engine; the +2 model has a number 2 after the FI – *viz*, FI2.

APPENDIX D

Production and deliveries

Helped by research into the various recording systems which TVR has employed in the last two decades, and by assistance from the Society of Motor Manufacturers and Traders, I believe this is an accurate summary of TVR production and deliveries since the Tasmin was put into production at the end of 1979. For interest, in the Annual Production section, the last two calendar years (1978 and 1979) *before* the Tasmin was introduced, are also included:

Annual production figures

Year	Total production	Home market	Export market
1978	310	164	146
1979	308	168	140
1980	144*	133	11
1981	164	146	18
1982	121	109	12
1983	291**	192	99
1984	397	162	235
1985	472	161	311
1986	396***	201	195
1987	322	225	97
1988	701	576	125
1989	715****	654****	61
1990	746	665	81
1991	719	645	74
1992	824	752	72

*   The year in which Tasmin production took over completely from the previous range.

**   Deliveries to the US market resumed.

***   The last year in which the US market took a large proportion of TVR production.

****   Includes 35 Tuscan race cars.

Total production of each model – from 1980

Model	Total production	By year
Tasmin S1	118	6 in 1979
		103 in 1980
		9 in 1981
Tasmin Convertible/280i	862	25 in 1980
		93 in 1981
		54 in 1982
		92 in 1983
		174 in 1984
		239 in 1985
		149 in 1986
		31 in 1987
		5 in 1988
Tasmin +2 Coupe	47	14 in 1980
		27 in 1981
		1 in 1982
		3 in 1983
		2 in 1985
Tasmin S2/280i Coupe	140	23 in 1981
		35 in 1982
		26 in 1983
		49 in 1984
		3 in 1985
		4 in 1987
Tasmin 200 Coupe	16	1 in 1981
		9 in 1982
		5 in 1983
		1 in 1984
Tasmin 200 Convertible	45	7 in 1981
		19 in 1982
		13 in 1983
		6 in 1984

Model	Total production	By year
350i Convertible	897	50 in 1983
		88 in 1984
		143 in 1985
		218 in 1986
		151 in 1987
		92 in 1988
		119 in 1989
		36 in 1990
350i Coupe	52	10 in 1983
		11 in 1984
		9 in 1985
		11 in 1986
		11 in 1987
350i +2 Coupe	6	5 in 1983
		1 in 1984
390SE/420SE Convertible	103	5 in 1984
		13 in 1985
		12 in 1986
		22 in 1987
		51 in 1988
400SE Convertible	242	15 in 1988
		102 in 1989
		81 in 1990
		44 in 1991
450SE Convertible	35	24 in 1989
		11 in 1990
420SEAC	37	4 in 1986
		14 in 1987
		19 in 1988
450SEAC	18	4 in 1988
		14 in 1989
S1 and S2 Roadster	2,048	1 in 1986
		89 in 1987
		515 in 1988
		421 in 1989
		618 in 1990
		404 in 1991

Model	Total production	By year
S3 and S3C Roadster	112	63 in 1991
		49 in 1992
S4C Roadster	32	32 in 1993 (Jan–June)
V8S Roadster	408	208 in 1991
		173 in 1992
		27 in 1993 (Jan–June)
Tuscan Race Car	45	35 in 1989
		6 in 1990
		4 in 1992
Griffith	704	602 in 1992
		102 in 1993 (Jan–June)
Chimaera	278	278 in 1993 (Jan–June)

Note: Detail figures have been included up to the end of June 1993 – halfway through the calendar year.

APPENDIX E

Performance figures for all models

Magazine road testers have always loved driving TVRs, so there was no shortage of raw material to compile this section. As usual in *Collector's Guides*, only tests conducted with accurate speed-recording instruments have been considered, and for the charts provided figures have been extracted from tests published since 1980 in *Autocar* (latterly *Autocar & Motor*).

Each test, I believe, represents the average 'as-new' performance of each TVR model, with its engine in standard condition. However, in the late Eighties/early Nineties TVR were always ready to provide engines with more power than standard, and alternative final-drive gearing was often available, so there may be some proud owners out there who insist that: "Mine's quicker than *that*…" – and they may be right.

	Tasmin S1 2,792cc V6/160bhp Ford	350i Series 2 3,528cc V8/197bhp Rover	390SE 3,905cc V8/275bhp Rover	420SEAC* Race car 4,228cc V8 Rover	S 2,792cc V6/160bhp Ford	V8S 3,950cc V8/240bhp Rover	Griffith 4,280cc V8/280bhp Rover	Tuscan** Race car 4,441cc V8 Rover
Mean maximum speed (mph)	130	136	144	147	128	146	161	157
Acceleration (sec)								
0–30mph	3.2	2.5	2.1	1.9	2.4	2.0	2.1	1.9
0–40mph	4.7	4.1	3.3	2.6	3.8	3.1	2.7	2.7
0–50mph	6.4	5.0	4.4	3.4	5.6	4.1	3.7	3.4
0–60mph	8.2	6.6	5.7	4.6	7.6	5.2	4.7	4.0
0–70mph	10.3	9.3	7.8	5.7	10.4	7.1	6.0	5.3
0–80mph	13.3	11.7	9.8	7.4	13.5	8.7	7.5	6.2
0–90mph	16.8	14.6	12.1	9.0	17.1	10.8	9.1	7.3
0–100mph	23.2	20.2	15.4	10.7	22.8	13.5	11.1	8.9
0–110mph	32.5	23.0	19.5	13.2	30.6	16.3	13.6	10.6
0–120mph	–	29.4	26.7	15.7	–	20.2	16.4	12.6
0–130mph	–	–	–	20.8	–	27.0	–	15.5
Standing ¼-mile (sec)	16.4	14.8	14.2	13.5	15.9	14.0	13.2	12.2
Top gear (sec)								
10–30mph	–	–	10.7	–	–	–	–	–
20–40mph	8.1	8.9	10.5	–	9.0	6.5	6.7	6.6
30–50mph	8.3	8.3	9.7	–	8.8	6.1	6.3	5.2
40–60mph	8.6	8.6	8.4	7.5	9.2	6.0	6.3	4.5
50–70mph	8.7	8.8	8.9	8.7	10.5	6.0	6.4	4.9
60–80mph	9.5	9.2	9.9	7.8	11.8	6.2	6.4	4.9
70–90mph	10.3	9.6	11.4	7.1	13.6	6.6	6.4	5.1
80–100mph	11.8	10.2	11.6	7.6	13.9	7.0	6.7	5.0
90–110mph	15.7	12.2	11.2	7.4	–	7.7	7.1	5.0
100–120mph	–	–	13.6	7.8	–	8.7	7.8	5.5
110–130mph	–	–	–	–	–	11.2	–	6.3
Overall fuel consumption (mpg)	21.6	19.6	16.6	n.q.	27.3	20.1	19.1	n.q.
Typical fuel consumption (mpg)	24	22	18	n.q.	30	n.q.	n.q.	n.q.
Kerb weight (lb)	2,562	2,520	2,678	n.q.	2,173	2,247	2,304	n.q.
Original test published	1980	1985	1987	1987	1987	1991	1992	1989

*   Fitted with a 365bhp engine. Other examples had a different power output.
** Fitted with a 348bhp engine. Other examples had even more power, some being quoted at 420bhp!
n.q. = not quoted.